MODEL-MAKING

Materials and Methods

MODEL-MAKING

Materials and Methods

DAVID NEAT

PHOTOGRAPHS BY ASTRID BÄRNDAL

THE CROWOOD PRESS

First published in 2008 by
The Crowood Press Ltd
Ramsbury, Marlborough
Wiltshire SN8 2HR

www.crowood.com

British Library Cataloguing-in-Publication Data
A catalogue record for this book is available from the British Library.
ISBN 978 1 84797 017 6

Dedication
This book is dedicated to: my parents, Barbara and Wilf,
my dear brother Tim,
and to Astrid, with also such gratitude for her expert help and patience.

Acknowledgements
Staff and students at Rose Bruford College, Kent and Wimbledon College of Art, London are
gratefully acknowledged, in particular Iona McLeish: Theatre Design Programme, Rose Bruford
College and Chris Dyer: Wimbledon College of Art. The author would also like to thank
4D Modelshop, London; the Arts Institute at Bournemouth and Martina von Holn.

Illustration credits
David Lazenby, Lazenby Design Associates (www.lazenbydesign.com), Astrid Bärndal
(www.baerndal.eu), Dragonfly Models (www.dragonflymodels.co.uk), Lizzie Oxby, Charlotte
Hern, Valerie Charlton, 4D Modelshop, London, Elves n Elements (www.elvesnelements.com),
Dick Bird, Ben Stones, John P. Hall (www.setsmachine.co.uk), David Burrows, Marie Antikainen,
Marc Steinmetz, Rachel Waterfield, Dee Conway, Richard Battye

All other photos are by Astrid Bärndal unless otherwise stated, as are all models by the author
unless otherwise indicated.

Disclaimer
The information given in this book is either tested through experience or to the author's best
knowledge, but neither the author nor the publisher can be held responsible for any resulting
injury, damage or loss to either persons or property. Efforts have been made to ensure safety
but the proper health and safety guidelines for each material featured should be consulted
independently.

Typeset by Jean Cussons Typesetting, Diss, Norfolk
Printed and bound in Singapore by Craft Print International Ltd

CONTENTS

CHAPTER 1

INTRODUCTION

The making of 'small forms'

In many ways, this book is about the making of 'small forms' regardless of their purpose. It is dedicated to providing technical assistance to those who, for whatever reason, have to work at that level of intricacy where the fingers (and perhaps also the brain!) find it difficult to cope. It considers the range of materials which could be used to make such small work, how these will behave and how those properties can be manipulated to make life easier. It is divided into chapters which follow the process of making; from planning and building, through ways of creating surfaces, to final painting and finish.

If this were a book about 'small sculpture', on the other hand, it would probably be more interested in artistic context. It might dwell more on the aesthetic qualities of form, the integrity of the medium and the longevity of the message. This book concerns itself far less with the question of what is created, more with the question of 'how'. It considers any material as worthy, however base, impure, cheap or discarded others might view it. It will hardly ever recommend a material for the purpose for which it was intended! It will be content to advocate a fragile and temporary lifespan as long as the outcome will perform for as long as it's meant to. Sometimes the real 'outcome' is not even the object itself, but the knowledge gained by making it; the discovery of the process.

Also, if this were a book about 'small sculpture', its bias towards realism might be off-putting. It encourages a slavish attention to how 'real things' look. It leaves abstraction, simplification or stylistic licence aside, as decisions for the individual, and considers them only insofar as they might enhance the sense of the real. In that sense, this book is quite traditional, believing that one can only convey truth by being firmly founded on the appearance of the real. But leaving that debate aside, the practical reason for staying with the real throughout these pages is simply that there is no better way for the reader to be able to judge the effectiveness of the examples and methods shown.

So, in its dedication to the effectiveness of the real, you'll find this book follows a fairly disciplined adherence to proportion and scale, not only for structures but also for textures, and suggests methods that will help in keeping to them. It advocates,

for example, using natural processes to mimic nature, making the materials do most of the work at a level of detail which usually defies the scalpel or the brush. It questions the assumptions we often make based on how we think something looks, rather than acknowledging what we are actually seeing or taking the trouble to find out.

REALISM

Reality is a universally shared language. Models can make full use of that, relying on that shared language for their effectiveness and appeal. A sense of how things *should* look is so embedded within all of us that we can be affected by the most subtle of changes or the slightest variance in scale without even being conscious of it. Yet the fact that this sense is so embedded may also be the reason why it is often so difficult to 'see' objectively what it is that makes something look so real and to recreate that quality in something artificial. That difficulty in consciously 'seeing' may explain why such a familiar form as the human head can become so elusive when we try to model it. Yet we are so fine-tuned in recognition of the essentials that we can spot the contours of a familiar face amongst a crowd of others at a surprising distance. Models make use of the fact that we all share a common awareness of how real things look, but they also benefit from the fact that we either don't look too closely, or are sometimes seduced by the superficial. The fact that we can be so easily fooled by the power of suggestion means that models may not have to work too hard to convince, as long as the essentials are wisely chosen. A small figure can often impress as 'realistic' if the proportions are convincing, even though the surface treatment or lack of detail may be unnatural. On the other hand, a nondescript form can often take on the appearance of something very real by adding carefully considered details. Sometimes the 'essentials' are in the form, sometimes in the details; most often they are provided by a combination of the two.

A final presentation model made by David Lazenby, whose company (Lazenby Design Associates) designs and builds environments for zoos, aquariums and museums. These models are taken to a high degree of detail and realism, enabling the fullest understanding of the intended design.

Who is this book for?

This book is intended for experienced students or beginner professionals in any discipline for which accurate scale models are required as part of the job. The bias is, admittedly, towards theatre or film model-making, because this is where most of my experience lies. But the range of model-making practised for the theatre and film can be viewed as a repository of knowledge for other fields such as architecture or interior design. By 'experienced students', I mean those who already have some understanding of scale, who are already fairly confident with a scalpel and who are looking for a guidebook rather than an instruction manual. But having said that, parts of this book have to be arranged like a manual simply because the techniques and material preferences of model-makers tend to become rather personal. Without a step-by-step account of some things, it might not be obvious what happens next! I have tried wherever possible to reflect recognized practice where it matters, but model-making is not exactly a long-established profession with its own regulatory guild and set of standards, so a book like this can't avoid being based more on personal experience than anything else.

This book also confines itself to what can be achieved by relatively simple means without the use of expensive equipment, making use of materials that are readily available and avoiding techniques which require a disproportionate amount of time or effort to master. It acknowledges that for most people

An unusually realistic exterior in 1:10 scale from Lizzie Oxby for her animated film, *Extn.21*. The underlying structure may be simple, but the attention given to the way surfaces are broken down by the elements and the often haphazard gathering of details are very persuasive.

model-making is a sporadic rather than continual practice and very few will be able to afford a dedicated workshop. It may tend towards the traditionalist view that machines can distance us from a full appreciation of material, however useful they might be. Certainly it draws inspiration from countless instances where the simplest solution to a problem has often proved the best. In attempting to be interdisciplinary while keeping the book to a reasonable size I have had to leave many specialist methods out of it, but my hope is that the common ground remaining will be useful for all model-makers, suggesting methods or materials which might be very familiar in one context but largely unknown in another.

How is this book arranged?

This book is divided into chapters which reflect the chronology of making, as far as is possible, so that it could conceivably be read from beginning to end to accompany a project. Building comes first and the approach is similar whether the outcome is a landscape or a chair. The same goes for creating the appropriate surface and applying the final colour. However, certain self-contained subjects such as casting, modelling or working with metals have demanded separate chapters and these are interspersed where most appropriate rather than appendixed at the end.

Cross-referencing with the Directory of Materials

In most of these chapters I have given a summary introduction to the subject area, followed by an overview of materials and methods considered, before dealing with step-by-step accounts of specific examples. The emphasis throughout is, as I have said, on materials, but rather than burden each chapter with long accounts of their properties I have consolidated these in the Directory of Materials at the end of the book. Each chapter therefore contains just enough information on materials to get by and to make sense of what follows, but more information (particularly on obtaining them, average cost and possible alternatives) may be contained in the Directory of Materials. For the same reasons, tools are not fully explained in the chapters unless this is necessary for the process being considered (and it is assumed that people will be familiar with the basic tools). The Directory will provide more information on these. In short, if you want information about a specific material or a tool first, you can find it in the Directory and then refer back to its featured uses. But if you are more interested in finding out about a process you should go to the relevant chapter first.

The purposes of models

Does a model need to be convincing? Yes – but that doesn't mean it has to fool! Conviction can be achieved by many different means according to the many different visual languages which models are expected to comply with. The question of what a model is, what its purpose is and what makes it effective will have to be answered differently according to the variety of disciplines in which models are used.

Models in the theatre

Theatre designers will habitually use two types of model in the process of designing a set for the stage (here the word theatre is used in the sense of 'anything taking place on a stage' and includes opera, dance and musicals). The first type is the rough, or 'sketch', model which the designer can put together relatively early in the process and which represents a quick mock-up of developing ideas. It is quite literally three-dimensional sketching, unfussy and exploratory. It may not even be intended for anyone else to see at first, although pretty soon it tends to become an essential tool during talks with the director. At this point it can be played around with, cut up or even bounced off the wall, hopefully without any feelings of resentment or wasted effort! Some designers may leap into cardboard straight away and not do any paper sketching at all, while others will try to put off the 3-D moment for as long as possible. Directors tend to appreciate seeing something tangibly spatial fairly early on in the process though.

Usually white or recycled card (basically anything scrap or *neutral* cheap) suffices for the sketch model stage. It may be a good *colour* idea to use something with a neutral colour such as recycled *sketch* board or even brown box cardboard, because stark white tends *es* to generate a false impression of space especially if the final *cardboard* treatment is likely to become dark.

Once the designer has reached some certainty with the design and those immediately involved in the collaborative process (such as director, lighting designer or choreographer) have been consulted for their input, the final model (the *sketch* second of the two mentioned) can begin. It may be that *1:50* the sketch models have been made at a smaller scale, for example 1:50, in the interests of speed. In this case, the final *final* model will be built (almost always 1:25 metric scale in the *1:25* UK) completely from scratch. It may also be that the designer has built the model box (a transportable model of the stage space in which the design is set including proscenium, orchestra pit and means of hanging flown scenery) in 1:25 and worked directly in this during the sketch-modelling process. Some elements of the sketch model may therefore

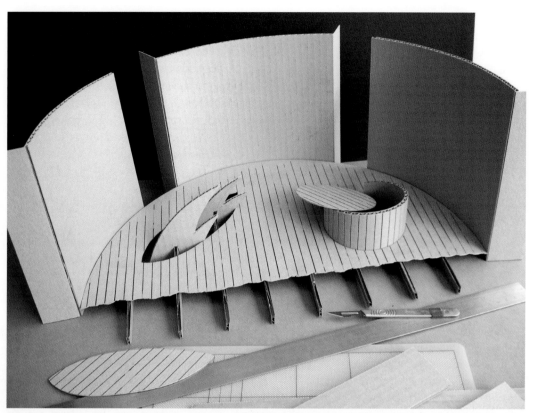

Sketch model for *The Tempest*. This is, if anything, unusually neat! The sketch model is an opportunity to play freely with shape, proportion and scale without being too 'precious' about the execution. It often helps if the materials chosen to do this are fairly poor to begin with. Photo: David Neat

BELOW: The final model. Even when refining an abstracted setting, a convincing scale in relation to the human figure is important. Photo: Dee Conway

be refined to serve as the final model. Whichever way, the distinction between 'sketch' and 'final' can sometimes be blurred.

Final set models for the theatre are most often taken to a very high level of detail, colour and textural finish. Scale and detail have to be consistent if the 'illusion' is to work, drawing the observer into an appreciation of a believable space. The problem with convincing scale is that it really has to be all or nothing. If trouble is taken to model wall mouldings or window struts with an accurate slenderness and profile, the same has to apply to chair legs, carpet texture and wallpaper pattern if the design includes these. To call a final theatre set model a 'presentation' model is not doing it full justice. It works hard from that point, selling the designer's idea and providing the

HOW A SET DESIGN MODEL WORKS

There are many good arguments why the theatre set model should convey the designer's intentions as accurately as possible and many justifications why the designer should focus so much of his or her effort on the model.

For the designer: the set design is a bit like a 3-D painting, visually balancing form, colour and texture, in addition to the all-important space. The model is the only way to appreciate fully how this might work together, for example the visual weight of furniture in the space, the difference in having a matt surface as opposed to a gloss. Secondly, the designer can use the process of building the model as an aid to understanding eventual construction, which will be of great benefit in technical discussion with the workshops.

For director and collaborators: (such as the lighting designer, choreographer) accuracy in scale will help them, particularly the director, to understand what kind of space they're looking at.

For scenic workshops: an important part of the designer's responsibility is to provide complete measured drawings for every element of the set or furniture that needs to be made. No one should use the model as a source of finite measurement, but the model will help greatly to clarify drawn information. It is almost certainly the primary source of information for the scenic artists whose job it is to paint and texture the set.

For the ensemble: actors will appreciate being presented with a true representation of the environment their character will inhabit on stage. Often the first time the designer meets the cast is at the model showing at the beginning of rehearsals. A well-crafted model helps to convince the ensemble that the designer knows what he or she is doing!

**Models intended for special effects are often made to merciless standards of precision and realism, especially where the subject may be familiar. This model of the entrance to the Grand Central Terminal in New York was made by Charlotte Hern while still a student of Modelmaking for Design and Media at the Arts Institute at Bournemouth.
Photo: Rachel Waterfield**

detailed information needed for the full-scale creation of the design. 'Working model' acquires a particularly apt second meaning in this case.

There is no absolute illusion possible when looking at a theatre set model. We know it's a model because we're standing there looking down at it. Even so, it helps to convince everyone involved if the model allows them just a little of that famous 'suspension of disbelief'. We could rate it as good, rather than just adequate or functional, if it inspires us with the feeling that we are looking at a real space, in which all the elements, whether large or minute, are rendered with such an attention to scale and surface quality that we can almost see real characters wandering around in it. This may be much more difficult if the concept is abstract, with fewer indications of real-life scale. Here it could be legitimately argued that, whereas it may well be the purpose of the actual set to convince as part of the theatrical illusion, it is unreasonable to expect it of the model. The model is, after all, not an end in itself, but just a means to an end. It may suffice that the model is a functional blueprint of the designer's intentions, perhaps supported by other reference material, and not a tour de force of miniaturist skill – no sensible scenic artist will assume that the smears of glue on a hastily painted piece of card are there to be recreated in full size! Well … surely not?

Models in film

When considering the use of models in film, one has first to separate three distinct areas: how models are used in the production design process; how models contribute to special effects; and the more specialized genre of stop-motion animation.

One would expect film production designers to make very similar use of models to theatre set designers. Both are responsible for creating spaces where action can happen and where characters can unfold. But there are more fundamental differences in the working process than there are correspondences. When working for film, sets are not usually minutely recreated in model form (that is, not for the purposes of the production process). Forms of model are necessary, and they are common practice, but they are most often made in unpainted card (so-called 'white card models') mainly to show the director, the cinematographer or the crew how much space there will be to work on set. These models are also useful in the early stages for budgeting.

There are reasons why it is just not feasible or relevant for the production designer (or rather the art department) to produce more detailed set models. The theatre set is a build for one location, that is, the theatre stage, which will be seen from just

A typical white card model. This is usually done directly from the technical drawings, pasted onto foamboard, to render a schematic but spatially accurate model of the intended set. Its purpose is practical rather than aesthetic and there is no need to recreate atmosphere. Photo: David Neat

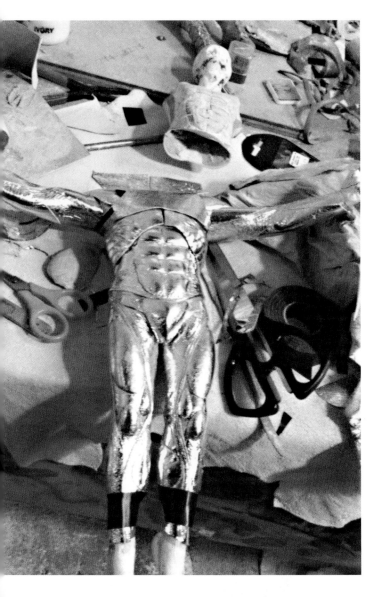

Three photographs illustrating Valerie Charlton's work on the flying model of Sam Lowry for a dream sequence in Terry Gilliam's *Brazil*. The first shows the model in progress, the second (left) shows it ready for filming and the third shows Jonathan Pryce as Sam Lowry in the same sequence.
Photos: Valerie Charlton

one viewpoint per audience member, making the single model relatively straightforward. Film is a different medium, with a multiplicity of viewpoints determined by the camera. There may be hundreds of locations, many of which do not need to be built and some of which might only be glimpsed out of focus over an actor's shoulder. The 'look' of a film is just as much determined by the temporal flow of images corresponding to the action and this can often be conveyed far better through the storyboard.

But the case is very different in the area of special effects. In spite of the phenomenal advances made in CG (computer-generated) techniques in recent years, models continue to be used in film and not just those with a low budget. Films such as *Master and Commander*, *Lord of the Rings*, *The Fifth Element*, *End of Days* and *Batman Returns* have all made extensive use of models, usually in conjunction with digital effects. Film-makers have used models creatively in film since the birth of the medium and some of the techniques employed in ground-breaking early films such as *Metropolis* (1927) are still common practice today.

Models are considered as an option in a wide variety of circumstances. Most obviously, where a landscape setting or buildings are entirely imaginary models can be made, filmed and, where necessary, live action can be merged using a variety of methods. Sometimes even when a setting exists or a set is built to full size, model versions may be used either to extend the apparent dimensions of these, or (where pyrotechnics have to be used) to avoid having to destroy the real thing. They can also play an uncredited supporting role in films where one would least expect them. Hitchcock's *Rope* for example, in which all the action takes place in an apartment room, features a large cityscape seen through the window. It is always there under scrutiny, but still manages to be convincing within the stylistic language of the drama.

Is a 'good' special effects model one which is crafted and filmed so skilfully that we have no consciousness of it being a model? It is much easier to deceive the camera than it is the eye, especially when it comes to space and scale, and the illusion can be greatly supported by careful lighting. The models can therefore be simple, seem even crude on close inspection, and often disappoint if they're exhibited outside the film. But there will be no error in scale or strangeness that would disturb the suspension of disbelief which we require to enjoy the film fully. The essentials of realism are well understood. Of course we know, in another part of our mind, that a fantasy landscape doesn't really exist! But, even so, the illusion is somehow strengthened if we nevertheless pretend in that same part of our mind that the film company has spared no expense to build a full-size environment.

The final category of models in film, that of stop-motion animation, is a very special form of film-making which has enjoyed a boost in recent years largely through the efforts of Tim Burton and Aardman Animations. For these films the model sets enjoy just as much loving attention, from makers and audience alike, as the puppet actors. As with special effects, models made for animation are almost the end products (awaiting transformation to film), rather than just meticulous blueprints for something else. Some animation sets are made with remarkable realism (such as the set from Lizzie Oxby shown earlier), but because it is more common for stop-motion puppets to be designed as caricatures, settings often take similar liberties with scale, proportion and colour. As with special effects models, much can be done with lighting and the inclusion of digital effects after filming. Because what counts is only what the camera can see, a whole range of temporary fixes (such as unseen Blu-Tack or Sellotape) can be employed.

These set models are often built to special requirements. The scale can normally be as much as 1:10, often larger, usually in accordance with the size of the puppet characters. The sets

One of Lizzie Oxby's sets for her film *Extn.21* on the animation 'table' showing the lights in position. The set has been built 1:5 scale.

Set models 1:10

The set as it appears in the film showing the effect of controlled lighting. The text on the miniature TV screen was added digitally during post-production.

often have to be made in sections that can be easily pulled apart so that camera viewpoint can be manipulated. This also enables the animators to get close enough to the figures to perform the painstaking sequence of operations needed to create the illusion of movement. Many of the large sets for Tim Burton's *The Nightmare Before Christmas,* for example, were fitted with trapdoors through which the animators had to squeeze to access the figures during some scenes. The figures also need to be secured to the base during this process, usually by means of holes drilled through the floor of the model through which the puppet feet are bolted. Normally this 'peppering' with holes will not be visible in the final shots. Another important requirement, with regard to the materials chosen, is that they can withstand the heat generated by the lights during filming.

Architectural models

Everyone will probably be familiar with the pristine representations of modern developments, unveiled at their launch and exhibited proudly in architects' offices.

They are designed to look as attractive and as clean as possible. This cleanliness is not part of an effort to preserve illusion; on the contrary, it helps to maintain the status of the model as a refined expression of the ideal. In a sense, architectural models strive to preserve the building as an idea in the imagination, while making it possible for others, such as clients, to share in the imagination of the architect. A 'good' architectural model created for boardroom presentation may show little trace of the human hand; indeed, the laser has replaced the scalpel for most intricate cutting (not just a practical move but somehow also a fittingly aesthetic one). The location is also simply represented, often abstracted, in order to focus on the essentials of the new form.

Stylistic liberties will be taken, rather than striving to represent the real materials – for example, cityscape models may be clad in expensive wood veneer rather than a more factual representation of something like concrete being attempted. The argument is, again, that by abstracting the surface the eye can concentrate more on the essential form. But the choice of material is also a form of flattery. The craftsmanship which is particularly evident in the finish of these models suggests that the client is worthy of pampering. Added to this, the viewpoint from which these models are judged is also quite a flattering one. No one will ever see the real building from such a 'God's eye viewpoint'! In the case of architectural model-making, the object is not so much to convince as to persuade.

What are perhaps not so familiar are the sketch models produced during the process, or those models whose purpose is to convey a general formal principle rather than the finished building. These are different in that the architects usually create them themselves in the early stages (rather than commissioning a specialist model-maker to work from the final plans). These are often improvised and playful, both in the manner of making and materials used, and that manner often extends to versions created for display. A recent exhibition of design development models included one form wrapped in

bandages secured with elastic bands and another one created in jelly!

Product simulation

This highly skilled and specialized area of model-making deserves a mention, even though this book can't cater specifically for it. Similar to commercial architectural model-making, product simulation tends to be a fast-track, machine-intensive affair, except more so! 'Rapid prototyping' is a term commonly used and would seem to sum it up nicely. The differences are that models for this purpose are often life size and look (and sometimes even feel) extremely real. Both architectural design and product simulation are more recognized (and also more suitably trained) than other forms of model-making, so materials and methods are more standardized. The emphasis on functionality leads to many of these models actually being made with moving parts, which gives yet another meaning to the phrase 'working model'.

The final model in product simulation is usually the last in a long line of design prototypes employing a variety of materials. Whether the model is durable or temporary depends on the uses to which it is then put and these can vary. Master models, from which dies will be made to manufacture the real thing, need to last. Other finished models intended just to be photographed for promotional purposes may not. But for most purposes the industrial precision and immaculate surfaces required demand similarly industrial techniques of shaping and finishing which are outside the scope of this book.

What makes good model-making?

Good model-making is not necessarily the same as achieving the end product of a good model. What is just as important as the quality of the final outcome is the efficiency of the process of getting there. This includes how sketch models are used to generate ideas, how materials are chosen to fulfil a particular task, how the workspace is arranged to work comfortably and how time is managed to ensure that important tasks get enough of it. Good professionals, in any discipline, tend to be extremely organized individuals!

The effective use of sketch models to explore design solutions requires a specially developed eye. The freedom is needed to manipulate materials quickly, concentrating on essentials of form and not being precious about their finish. It may be a good idea habitually to make sketch models out of the same material, just as an artist has a favoured form of sketchbook, so that one can get accustomed to their language. On the other

Architectural models are often faultless in their representation of structure. This is a detail of a 1:50 scale model made by Dragonfly Models, Worcestershire, for Glenn Howells Architects. Photo: by Richard Battye

These models display a particular aesthetic (or visual language) of their own which became a recognized standard during the last century. Model by Dragonfly Models for Immodicus Design Ltd. Photo: Jeanette Wieckhorst

hand, different materials can facilitate different shapes and inspire new design possibilities, so that 'disciplined eye' also needs to be free to rove. Especially in the later stages of model-making success depends on knowing what might be possible with a wide variety of materials, rather than being confined to a few. It may be most practical to limit one's experience to the familiar and the available, but all too often design decisions are then made according to what's possible in the model rather than what's best for the design.

Some might say that the most valuable, flexible and least understood material that the model-maker must learn to use is not cardboard, wood or plastic … but time! Contrary to the popular assumption, time can be manipulated, or at the very least 'saved', and many labour-saving methods and tools will be considered, particularly in Chapter 2, 'Constructing'. It is

important to use these as cues in developing one's own critical attitude towards the demands of the work, always being on the lookout for less laborious solutions without compromising either freedom or quality. It is easy to become seduced by the therapeutic nature of some model-making tasks. They can often be used (and needlessly extended!) in avoidance of more important problems. If model-making is to remain effective, the time spent on a particular aspect must stay in proportion to its importance within the whole.

As a final word here, many might assume that only those who can work precisely with their hands will prove to be good model-makers. Certainly this ability is valuable, but perhaps even more vital are a discerning eye, a forager's mentality and a passion for problem-solving. Effective model-making is practised more in the head than in the hands!

- work well with hands ·
- Discerning eye·
- foragers mentality·
- passion for problem solving·

Knowing which out of an array of ready-made materials / forms can be utilized to make the job easier or quicker.
→ These areas mark the skill of a model-maker.

CONSTRUCTING

Model-making generally involves processes of construction rather than methods of sculpting. Raw materials are chosen which have already undergone some degree of formation, into sheets of a set thickness, or into strips, rods or tubes. Much of the model-maker's initial skill resides in knowing which available materials would be most suitable for a given task. This suitability includes factors such as: which can be cut or shaped appropriately to the forms required or in the time available; which are cost-effective (even an expensive material can save money when weighed against a saving of time or effort); how easy they are to join or bond; whether they can be appropriately surfaced or painted; how durable they are against use or transportation; or if any permanency is intended. But added to this technical knowledge is a different kind of creative expertise that involves knowing or intuiting which out of an infinite array of ready-made forms can be utilized to make the job easier or quicker. It is these areas of knowledge and creativity which mark the skill of a model-maker, far more than any manual ability.

This chapter focuses on three distinct material types, each with different properties – card, plastic and foam. Wood is given some consideration here (using the constructional example of making a panelled door), but its usefulness in model-making lies more in the area of surfacing. It is therefore featured more in Chapter 6, 'Creating Surfaces'. Whichever material one chooses to use, some general building guidelines can be applied to all.

Guidelines for starting

Planning

The importance of this first essential step can't be repeated often enough. It involves having some initial idea of how a chosen material will behave and planning construction accordingly. It also involves having a fairly clear idea ahead of time how surfaces or painting will be achieved so that the right basic materials are chosen and so that any extra thickness added later

is taken into account from the beginning. In addition, it makes sense to plan the construction so that individual pieces can be worked on flat (details built up, texture applied and painted) before being stuck together. Otherwise, it's very difficult to achieve the kind of finish you want in a corner that's difficult to get to with a brush!

Initial planning should also involve working out (as far as possible) the dimensions of each component part and compositing them on the sheet so that only half as many cuts need to be made and the material spared. This may seem rather too much micro-organization, but any decision that saves a little time will help in the end. The final stage of model-making is rarely a free-fall experience, such as modelling an abstract form in clay where the outcome is not yet known and the material remains flexible. Often the goal is minutely predetermined from the beginning and is just a case of copying in scale. All the dimensions are known or can be found. Planning is in this context not a straitjacket on creative freedom, but an insurance which should free time and mind to dwell on 'higher things'! As suggested in the Introduction, since model-making is most often a means to an end rather than the end in itself, 'effective' is not only what looks good, well-made or convincing, but what has served the process of getting there. If the final model has taken a disproportionate amount of time to complete at the cost of other things (though it may well do anyway!), it has ceased to be a proper team-player.

• hard point pencil — 2H —for measurement purposes.

Marking out and cutting

The following are some basic points which may be obvious to many, but are worth repeating here.

A hard pencil point should be used (for example, 2H) to make something between a dot and a dash to mark a measurement (a dot may be easily lost or mistaken, whereas a long dash can be inaccurate). When ruling a pencil line between points, your working light should fall towards the working edge of the (metal) ruler rather than creating a shadow. A pencil will never draw a line exactly on the metal edge, so you need to develop a feel for the right compensation; the same will apply

Using a small engineer's try square as an aid to marking out. This simple tool can save a lot of time.

[handwritten margin notes, right side, largely illegible] When material is thick eg. foam board — use try square — cut on one side / then again on other — cuts clean on further • always cut on same side of line)

[handwritten margin notes, left side] • large circles — blade at more oblique angle (parallel.) • tight circles / curve — blade more vertical

CUTTING CIRCLES

Circles or curves present a problem in any material. The less resistant the material, the easier it will be to cut them. The more pressure one has to exert on the knife, the more difficult it is to maintain the steady flow of the hand movement needed to keep the curve smooth to the line. It is essential to make the first run with the blade just a light scratch, as it were, to serve as a guide for the second where one can press harder. It may take three or four runs, but it is never a good idea to try to cut through anything manually in one go. For large circles, keep the blade at an oblique angle, that is, more parallel to the surface, because the length of blade will act as a smoothing guide for the line. If the curve is tight, the opposite is true and the scalpel has to be held more vertically. The gadgets sold to attach to a compass to cut a perfect circle may be fine for laying a guiding line, but it will be impossible to exert enough pressure this way to cut right through card or plastic.

(often more so) when using a blade. Placing masking tape along the underside of a flat metal ruler will help it to grip better. Many professionals mount their material on a drawing board for marking out, which saves a lot of time and effort in establishing steady lines and correct right angles. If this is not possible, a good try square will prove essential.

Carpenters will always hatch pencil lines on the side they don't want and doing a similar thing avoids confusion if you've marked out a number of shapes on one piece. Always try to cut on the same side of every line, even though this means having to rotate the sheet material often. This will help to maintain accuracy. Where the material is thick but still manageable with a knife (such as foamboard or foamed PVC sheet), it is easier to cut part-way on one side and cut the rest of the way on the other side (having extended the lines accurately round using the try square). This is not only a preferable method because the friction on the blade is halved, but also a perpendicular cut is easier to obtain.

Assembling

When assembling a model, the main concern is, at the risk of

Using a straight-sided
metal block as a
construction guide.

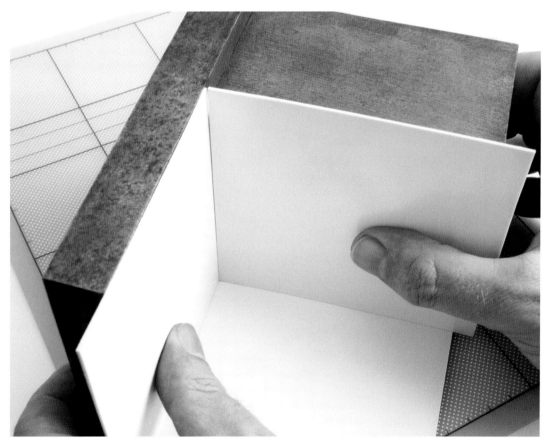

Two blocks aligned to
help with a corner.

stating the obvious, gluing in exactly the right place and maintaining that position until the glue is at least partially set. PVA and superglue are opposites in this respect. When using PVA or any slow-setting adhesive, there is some room for repositioning so that a part could almost be slid slowly into place if need be. Once there, it usually has to be secured by some means because it needs time to take hold firmly. With superglue, on the other hand, there is no chance for repositioning because it will bond immediately, but at least it will need no further assistance. Following are some guidelines that will help.

Instead of trying to align two edges of card by eye to form a right angle, such as a wall piece joined to the edge of a floor piece for example, turn the work over so that the wall piece rests flat on the work surface, then butt the floor piece up to it using the work surface as a stop while gluing. To avoid gluing to the work surface, put a piece of thin scrap paper underneath. This can be detached later and any small bits of paper that have become glued to the back can be sanded using a fine sanding block if necessary. A more versatile extension of using flat surfaces as guides or stops is to invest in some right-angled metal blocks.

The photos here show firstly how one of these blocks can help when gluing a right angle and then how two of these can assist in aligning the edges of a corner construction while gluing. These blocks need to be solid and weighty (so that they will not shift when pressed against) and the sides must be perfectly squared. The blocks shown here came as offcuts from a metal workshop and unfortunately are not available ready made in the shops, although they can be ordered from any firm willing to custom-cut metal.

An alternative is to make something like the assembly rig shown in the photo. It consists simply of two perpendicular walls attached to a firm baseboard. Thick MDF is an ideal choice here because of its smooth surface and it can be custom-cut by a timber merchant. All you need to do is to clamp the walls down while gluing, making sure that these remain at 90 degrees. The holes in the base are optional; they provide access for clamps if needed. The surface of the MDF should be kept clean and smooth. Paper should be inserted between the wood and anything being assembled so as to prevent gluing to the rig. An improvement would be to seal the surface with a tough polyurethane varnish.

"Assembly Rig"

A custom-made assembly rig in MDF.

More on gluing

More specific information on individual glues and their uses can be found in the Directory of Materials under 'Adhesives and solvents' but a number of things are worth summarizing here. A general point that tends to be forgotten is the 'less is more' principle. The tighter the fit between the two parts being joined, the less gap-filling the glue has to be. The bond will be stronger and it will take less time to set.

The nozzle of a PVA bottle, for example, tends to condition us into thinking that this is how the glue should be applied. The thickness dispensed in this way may be exactly right when gluing and clamping wood, but far too much along an edge of card. It helps sometimes to thin the glue slightly with water and apply it with a brush instead, although this is understandably less convenient. Either that, or one should dab the edge with the finger to even the glue out and take off some of the excess.

Solvent-based tube glues such as UHU may also be convenient for some things but are notoriously difficult to control and not really suitable for fine, clean work. Unlike PVA, which contracts to almost nothing as it dries, these glues will always leave an unsightly residue. An exception might be using solvent-based tubes for contact gluing. Here, the glue is applied to both surfaces and left for a little while. During this pause the glue can be evened out, with the finger as before or with a stick of card. After a few minutes, the surfaces will be dry to the touch but will bond firmly when pressed together under pressure. This must be done in the right place first time, because, although the bond will be rubbery and flexible until the glue hardens more, it is not possible to reposition.

Another very clean method of bonding which can be considered is to use double-sided tape. For laminating (joining two flat surfaces) large areas of card or plastic this can be a quick alternative to contact gluing as long as those surfaces are flat and clean. Only small squares of tape need to be distributed at key points. Also, for attaching clear acetate to the backs of window frames, small strips of tape around the outer edge are ideal. Double-sided tape can even be used in fine strips on foamboard edges to assemble a construction together provisionally. Sometimes this will hold for years, but it depends on the atmosphere and it can loosen if it gets too hot or humid.

Constructional examples

The following examples suggest ways to solve some common constructional problems, but it is not assumed that the solutions given here will be the only ones. There is no single right way of approaching something and a lot depends upon personal preference.

The parts of a chair drawn up at 1:10 scale with finished chairs at 1:25.

A simple chair

The example of making a simple chair has been chosen because it will be familiar to most. It is often assumed that the only way to build something of this delicacy properly is to take a ready made strip of an appropriate thickness in scale (for example, wood, or styrene) and painstakingly to assemble minute lengths together. This will, of course, work, but it is hard to keep such a minute construction straight and it will be fragile. The alternative approach suggested here is first to make fine cut-outs or silhouettes in a thin, stable material and then build upon them, adding strips to make up the right thickness. Foamed PVC is ideal for this method and more will be explained about this material later.

1. The first task is to draw up the parts of the chair (back, seat and front legs) on paper. In this case, the chair is 1:25 scale, but it is much easier to draw in a larger scale (1:10), then reduce the drawing (40 per cent) on a photocopier.
2. The reduced photocopy is then pasted onto 1mm foamed PVC. Spray Mount is best for this, although Pritt Stick could also be used, being careful to spread the glue evenly.
3. The parts of the chair can then be carefully cut out, through the photocopy and PVC. Foamed PVC is in many respects easier to cut than card, because there is less friction on the blade. It may not seem so at first though. If using this material for the first time it is important just to practise cutting it for a while, getting used to how much

The chair parts being cut out. Using a very small metal ruler will help. A strip of masking tape has been stuck to the underside to make the ruler grip better. The best knife to use is a surgical scalpel (*see* 'Tools' in the 'Directory of Materials').

A thickened chair compared to the flat version. The other advantage of using plastic cut-outs as a basis is that more fluid, ornamental shapes are possible.

AVOIDING CUTTING TOO FAR

When cutting anything like repeated windows in a shape the danger is always cutting too far (for example, cutting through a strut you want to keep), because you can't see where you're ending with the scalpel. One way of avoiding this is to cut all lines in one direction towards you first, stopping slightly short of the end of the line nearest to you. Turn the work right round and then complete the line from the other direction. Get into the habit of always cutting on the same side of the ruler. This will gradually help you to cut in the right place on a line each time.

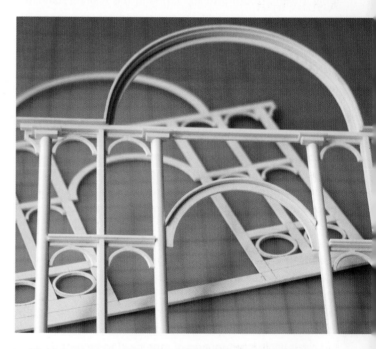

Work in progress. This piece of glasshouse architecture is being constructed in the same way as the chair, building thicknesses and profiles on a flat template.

pressure is needed. When cutting small components like this it is better to keep them in place (still contained within the surrounding plastic) until all lines have been cut. This helps to keep cut lines straight.

4. Once the parts have been cut out they can be glued together as they are, but this will make a rather insubstantial chair. At least the legs and outer frame should have thin strips of PVC added. It is much easier to add to a firm template in this way than to piece together from scratch. Superglue has to be used with this type of PVC. The paper photocopy can be left where it is if it is still firmly stuck, otherwise it can be peeled away from the plastic. If edges

*PVC. — Spray primer fot before acrylic pant.
* Stair — 2 piece / side with profile. top

still seem rough or uneven, the plastic can be sanded with fine sandpaper – disposable cardboard nail files are ideal for this kind of work.

5. Although the plastic will accept some acrylic paints, it is better to use a spray primer with them first. Enamel paint can be used without the need for a primer. The painted chairs in the first photo were given a base colour of Humbrol enamel and then rubbed with coloured pencil. The plastic for the seats was first scraped with coarse sandpaper (before being cut out) to simulate wood grain. These techniques are dealt with in Chapter 6, 'Creating Surfaces' and Chapter 7, 'Painting'.

A stair unit

Deciding how to make stairs is an exercise in spatial thinking. Making a wall with a window or a door in it does not involve such a leap into space, in that one can think more clearly in terms of two-dimensional layers. There is the main one representing the wall surface with the appropriate holes cut in it, then there are whatever layers are required to build up frames or mouldings on the front, and whatever layers are required behind to indicate the thickness of the wall. The basis is a flat cut-out onto which everything else is applied, either on one side or the other. But steps need to be approached differently. They are too deep to build in layers and it helps to visualize them more from the side as a solid box with a profiled top.

1. The first place to start is with the profile and two identical ones are needed. Having worked out the riser and tread (the height and the depth of each) for each step, a grid-work of rectangles with these proportions can be drawn on card, using the drawing board or try square to keep them straight. It is better to do this first as a grid to maintain a check on the right spacing, rather than build up an isolated zigzag. Also, these extended lines will serve as a better guide for the ruler when cutting. The profile can then be cut out, as shown. If one is careful to keep to the line and enough space has been left above, the waste zigzag can be used for the second profile. The grid lines will help in matching up.

2. When these have been done (and one has checked that they match), the best way of ensuring a straight and stable construction is to put them on a base. Cut a strip of card long enough to make both the base and all the tops of the treads. This is where some forethought comes in. If the profiles are glued to a base and the treads sit on top of the profiles, the top of the unit (and the first step) will be two thicknesses higher than it should be. The equivalent amount needs to be taken from the bottom of the profiles

Step profiles drawn and cut out. If cut accurately enough, the same zigzag can be used for both.

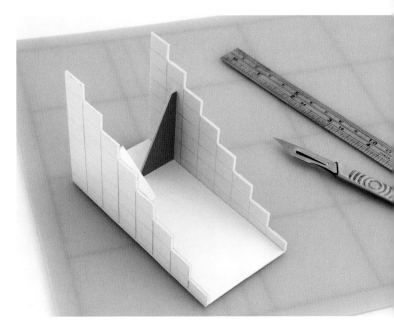

A base is important for keeping the construction together, but the extra thickness needs to be allowed for. Right angles help to keep the sides straight.

to compensate. Having done this, the profiles can be stuck to the base, including right-angled pieces to keep them straight. The assembly rig would be useful here for alignment of the parts.

3. The tops of the treads can be cut from the same strip used for the base, making them all the right length. But these are put aside for the moment because it is easier to glue

The risers are then
glued in place.

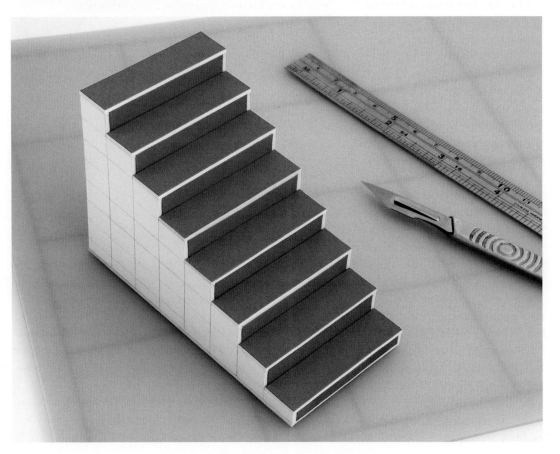

The completed stair unit.

the risers in first. These will have to be shorter (by two thicknesses of card) to sit between the profiles. The easiest way is to cut a strip (like the one for the base and treads) and test this for width before dividing it up with the try square. PVA should be used for any gluing of card. This stays repositionable for a short while, so the flat of the metal ruler can be used in this case to push the risers level.

4. All that remains is to glue the treads in place, which is simple since all the supports are already there. If the unit needs to be treated to suggest a particular material, it is far better to clad it with a prepared surface than painting or texturing the card directly. Similarly, if wooden stairs are needed, cladding is simpler than constructing the whole thing in wood, although the extra thickness needs to be planned for.

A panelled door

This is again more a case of building up layers of an appropriate thickness rather than constructing. Obeche wood is ideal in this case because it is thin, flat and easy to cut.

1. Having drawn up the door (even the simplest things should be worked out on paper first, especially if they are being designed as you go; these paper records will also be invaluable for the future), the base layer can be cut from obeche sheet. Parts of this will be visible as the interiors of the panels.

2. Strips of obeche are then added to this base to form the framework around the panels. Because obeche (like any thin wood or card) will warp if too much water-based glue is used it is better to spot PVA on the parts to be glued rather than spreading it. Only minute spots are necessary here to hold the strips firmly in place. Care needs to be taken to keep the glue from visible surfaces if the wood is going to be stained later. It is also worth remembering that, for both decorative and real-life structural reasons, grain usually follows length.

3. In this case, delicate profile strips were inserted, following the edge of each panel, to complete the effect. This is painstaking work at its best, but worth it for the overall effect. It is, of course, best to make up a longer length of profile strip and cut it up as necessary, rather than making each individually. Also, rather than trying to glue two delicate strips together after cutting them both out, it is easier to cut the smaller strip first and glue it to the edge of a larger sheet. Once the glue has set, the bottom strip, with the smaller strip already attached, can be cut off the sheet. For gluing thin elements like this, PVA should be thinned with a little water and applied sparingly with a very fine brush or the end of a cocktail stick.

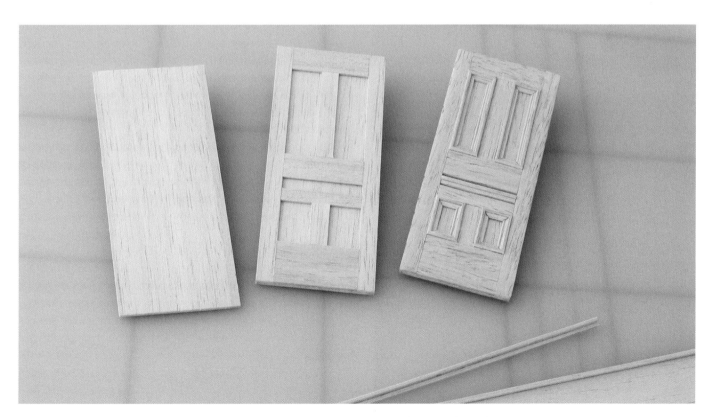

Three stages in building a door: base layer, framework, profile strips.

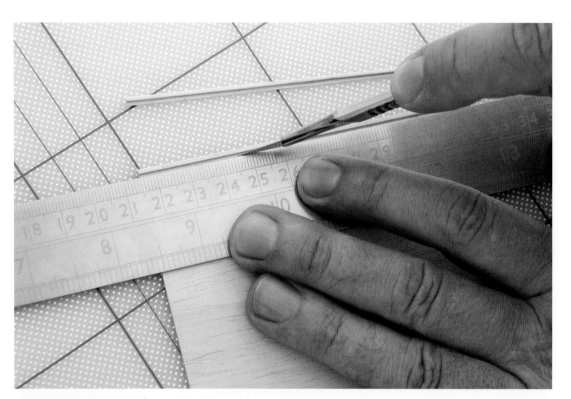

Cutting a profile strip.

BELOW: The finished door has been stained and waxed to emphasize the grain.

Working with card

Cardboard has always been a staple material, at least in theatre model-making and for other forms of a temporary nature. It will never become fully outdated, but as newer materials become more available its effectiveness should be questioned. Its main advantages remain that it is readily available in a variety of forms, is relatively cheap and is easy to cut with the simplest of tools. Its advantages become such a factor when faced with a tight deadline that many just accept or ignore its disadvantages without further question.

Cardboard of any kind has to be treated with care, that is, properly primed or sealed before it can be textured or painted. If not, it will warp badly! In fact, cardboard is so sensitive to atmospheric moisture or changes of temperature that it is usually bent before it gets to us. Ironically, despite its readiness to bend in this way it will not bend well when we want it to! It can be cut easily enough, but it can't be shaped and its edges can't be sanded in the way that those of wood can. Being absorbent, cardboard responds well to most glues, but as it is composed of layers this bond is only as strong as the outer layer and this is usually not very strong at all. Lastly, these layers will tend to separate when cut into thin shapes, making it unsuitable for any fine or detailed work.

Having listed all the disadvantages, it must be noted that the various forms of cardboard do have many useful qualities. The constructions featured here are works in progress which have been left unfinished to show the material and how the forms

Constructions in card. The most commonly used are mountboard and foamboard, but thinner types such as stencil paper are invaluable for finer work.

are put together. The scale used for all of these is 1:25. The various forms of cardboard and how to work with them are listed below.

 # Mountboard ⇒ Theatre Sets

Mountboard

This is the most commonly used card for theatre set models. Like almost everything else, it has been appropriated by model-makers but was never intended for them. It is intended mainly for passepartouts (cut-out windows for framing pictures under glass), hence the range of pastel colours available. This has also determined its consistency and softness so that it can be cut fairly easily at a slant to form what is known as a chamfered edge. The surface is smooth and matt on both sides, one being covered with a slightly tougher coloured paper while the other is left white. Theatre designers tend to favour the standard black/white version as an all-purpose material because the black side can also be used for theatre model boxes or to convey black masking in the set model. If other colours are used and intended to be kept as the wall colour, bear in mind that the surface can be very susceptible to grease marks while handling. It may be better, especially if mouldings need to be applied to the surface, to take the white side and paint it once all the gluing has been done.

**Showing strengtheners on the back of a mountboard construction. If mountboard is carefully scored halfway through, it can be made to follow a curve.**

Curving Mountboard #

THE PROBLEM OF WARPING

Sometimes the strengthening framework illustrated in the photo is enough. It should go without saying that this should be done after the wall piece is finished (the example shown may be confusing in this respect, but it is left unfinished to show the materials). If the card warps after painting it is often possible to ease it back straight enough for the backing to do the rest. Mountboard has an advantage here because the harder, coarser kind of card known as greyboard will be much more difficult to straighten by hand. It is, incidentally, completely false to assume that the thicker the card, the less it will warp. All it means is that once it does warp it will be almost impossible to straighten! Sometimes, therefore, it will make sense to work on very thin card, or even thick paper, before remounting it (preferably using Spray Mount) onto normal card.

The other ways of combating warping have to do with methods of painting, or types of paint, and are considered in Chapter 7, 'Painting'. Basically, either one can choose a spirit-based rather than a water-based paint, which will not usually affect the card, or one will have to prime or seal everything before painting. One slight advantage in using mountboard is that the coloured side is generally less absorbent, so if it is going to be painted it should be done on this side.

If used as a basis for building walls in the model, this material will hold up well enough but needs a lot of support. It will never be enough on its own and the photo illustrates the kind of framework needed on the back to keep it straight. It should not be necessary to buy wood for this because strips of card applied on edge will be surprisingly strong, unless the card has become so warped, for whatever reason, that something more forcible is needed.

Making strip mouldings and using a mitre guide

Some of the profiled mouldings (decorative strips) in these examples were made as longer strips which then had to be cut down, for example to form the doorframe. There is a limit to the detail or shape achievable with cardboard (see the later section on plastics in this chapter for other possibilities), but the way that cardboard and plastic are put together is the same. They are built up in layers of different width and thickness to approximate the effect needed. Each strip has to be cut separately, but rather than aligning them by eye while gluing, the handy metal block can be used as a guide.

Once ready, the strips have to be mitred in the case of the doorframe (the end cut at 45 degrees) to fit around a right angle, just like a picture frame. Mitre guides can be bought for carpentry, although they are far too big to serve here. It is necessary to make one's own mini version. The one shown here has been made from sheet PVC so that it will last. All that is

Making a profile strip for a doorframe using the metal block as a straight edge to glue against.

This custom mitre guide has been made especially for very small-scale work out of sheet PVC. It consists of two strips with angled ends, glued to a base. The work to be cut is positioned between them and the angles form a guide for the blade.

A collection of forms in stencil paper. The window frames at the back were cut from a continuous sheet to which mountboard elements have been added. Very delicate cut-outs are possible, remaining surprisingly strong, especially if supported.

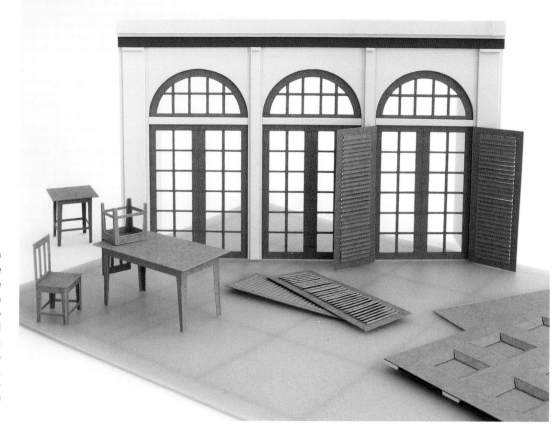

Small chairs made from stencil paper. The back and seat are cut separately, but the legs are a continuous strip that is scored and bent before gluing together with PVA.

needed is a means of guiding the blade to make a cut at a consistent 45-degree angle.

Parts of the mountboard wall featured here are curved. If card needs to be bent into a curve the only way to ensure a controlled, even bend is to make closely spaced, parallel cuts halfway through the card, as illustrated in the photo. This needs to be done on the side which will curve outwards. Once this curve has been secured in place, usually by backing it with curved supports, thinner card or paper will need to be glued onto the scored face for an even finish.

Stencil paper

This is more a thin card than a paper and is also known as oiled manila, but stencil paper is the name you'll usually find it by. It is used for cutting fairly durable stencils for decorative painting. The linseed oil which impregnates the card gives it a distinctive and thoroughly traditional smell. It also determines the colour, which ranges from light ochre to nut brown. It will cut very cleanly with no fray and maintains its straightness even after

Complicated structures can be achieved sometimes just by cutting and bending. Here, window shutters can be created by slitting the stencil paper in the right places and carefully bending the strips into a slant.

painting with thin acrylic. The waxy nature will ensure a very smooth cut even on small or compound curves because it offers less resistance to the blade. The oil prevents water from soaking in, but, surprisingly, PVA will work perfectly well to glue it.

Stencil paper responds well to scoring and bending while still retaining surprising rigidity for card so thin. The constructions shown here make use of that. For example, the heavy panelling was not made by gluing layers together but by scoring, cutting and bending single sheets. Achieving it this way can be quicker and the layout is kept more precise, although there is a limit to the intricacy possible with this cut-out method. Having said that, the delicate window shutters are an example of achieving an effect by this method which would otherwise be very time-consuming to construct in a conventional way. They are made by cutting lines through the stencil paper and bending each strip into a slant. The form is surprisingly stable. The distinctive colour of oiled manila can be used to good effect when simulating wood and may only need a little darkening. It will accept stain or ink reasonably well, although it is better if these are spirit-based. The subject of treatment is taken up again in Chapter 6, 'Creating Surfaces'.

Working with plastics

Plastics have been the materials of choice in architectural or product model-making for many years now, most often in sheet or strip form. Theatre designers, on the other hand, are only just beginning to consider them. The big advantage of plastics in commercial model-making is a combination of durability, workability and speed. As the technology produces more and more different types with different properties, so more of them filter down to craft and DIY shops and become accessible to model-makers.

Sheet plastics are much more robust than card and yet they are also flexible, allowing bending or shaping in ways that card cannot. Dependant on type, most are impervious to water or other solvents, so they won't warp when painted or textured and are unaffected by atmospheric conditions. They can also be tooled in a variety of ways, for example carved, lathed, sanded or impressed. Some of them, such as foamed PVC, are easier to cut with a knife than card of equivalent thickness and much finer detail is possible without the material disintegrating under the scalpel. Bonding is easy, whether using plastic solvent or superglue. The bond is immediate and very strong; no time is lost in waiting for glue to set before continuing. There may be less freedom for repositioning, but that contributes to a good alertness training!

Against these many advantages the drawbacks seem a bit paltry, but they are enough to put off a lot of people. Neither superglue nor plastic solvent are particularly pleasant to have around and good ventilation is essential. In addition, only a few types of plastic may be available, if you're lucky, at the local art

Dedicated professional stores such as the 4D Modelshop in London offer an invaluable range of materials at a glance. There is no better way to start learning about materials than simply to spend a bit of time browsing. Photo: courtesy 4D Modelshop.

Constructions using foamed PVC and styrene.

The examples shown here were made especially to illustrate the advantages of plastic over card. The glasshouse structure has already been referred to in the photos above. The materials used were foamed PVC sheet, thin sheet styrene and preformed styrene strip, all in common use. These materials are focused on here while information on other useful plastics (such as ABS, acetate or polypropylene) can be found in the Directory of Materials.

PVC

The work of the model-maker has been greatly eased in recent years (perhaps even revolutionized) by the invention of one form of plastic in particular: foamed PVC (Polyvinyl Chloride) sheet. The fact that it is 'foamed' is significant, to differentiate it from normal PVC sheet which is too dense for model-making purposes. This type of PVC was developed mainly as a lightweight, weather-resistant alternative to sheet wood for the production of signage. It is lightweight because it consists of an aerated centre closed by a smooth, impenetrable layer on both sides. This structure gives it its rigidity, acting in much the same way as a cross-strutted girder, but it also makes it very easy to cut. Because the surface will 'give' ever so slightly under the knife, there is less likelihood of the knife blade slipping and the absence of grain will ensure a smooth, even cut. Cut edges can also be filed or sanded very easily. All these qualities enable the kind of sharpness and precision illustrated in the photo. It is available not only in white but also in a range of colours and also a range of thicknesses from 1mm to 18mm. It can be found under a variety of brand names such as 'Foamex', 'Forex' or 'Foamalux' in shops specializing in plastics or display materials.

Superglue will form a strong, almost unbreakable bond with foamed PVC, but it can also be glued using a form of solvent which plumbers use for 'welding' PVC pipes together. The example of the chair construction at the beginning of the chapter illustrates how useful it is for making fine but stable constructions. 1mm PVC measures just 2.5cm (1in) at 1:25 scale, for example making it a much better scale choice than mountboard for structures such as furniture or window frames. Unlike mountboard, it can be sanded easily for either a sharp finish or a softer edge as required. Because the surface will 'give' slightly, it can be embossed easily with any sharp tool and given a grain effect with coarse sandpaper. For the same reason it scores and bends without breaking.

Styrene

Sheet styrene has similar properties but is denser and not

shop. A professional model shop such as 4D in London will have many of them and it is worth visiting just to acquaint oneself with the range. But for other types, such as foamed PVC, one has to locate a plastics specialist. Some of these are listed at the end of this book. Many people assume that plastic will be more expensive than card. Some types are, such as clear Perspex or acrylic, but others, such as foamed PVC or styrene, generally work out cheaper as long as one accepts having to buy a little more than one needs at the time. It is also assumed that plastic will be more difficult to paint, which is only partially true. Surfaces will certainly need priming first if thin washes are intended, but acrylic from the tube will take quite readily to PVC or styrene, especially if these are lightly sanded first. A full account of the various methods of painting is given in Chapter 7, 'Painting'.

Wall thicknesses for the curved windows of the façade were faced with styrene strips.

BELOW: A curved wall of styrene is first taped into position between weights. Solvent can then be applied from the outside using a fine brush. The plastic will weld, leaving little trace on the outside. This will only work when gluing styrene to styrene.

Composite profiles can be built up using preformed styrene strip.

CUTTING STYRENE

When cutting sheet styrene, care must be taken when making an initial cut because the blade will easily slip. Often it is better to sand with a fine sandpaper first to provide a key. It is difficult to mark lines properly with a pencil unless this is done. Alternatively, if you want to keep the surface shiny and unmarked you can cover areas to be cut with masking tape and mark out, or spray-mount a photocopy and cut through that. The metal rule will then grip a lot better. Afterwards, the tape or paper can be peeled away. Because it is slightly brittle, styrene can also be scored and snapped to produce a clean break. These are also good methods for marking and cutting clear plastics such as acetate or thin acrylic.

foamed. Styrene 1mm thick would be much more difficult to cut than the same thickness in foamed PVC. It is most often used in thinner forms (0.5mm, 0.25mm). Whereas PVC maintains its rigidity very well, styrene is much more bendable. It can be made even more malleable with heat (styrene is commonly used in vacuum forming). It will glue just as well with superglue, but can also be welded together using a solvent.

These chairs were also made from styrene strips. Styrene can be carved with the scalpel and sanded, achieving fine detail. Photo: David Neat

Finished chairs. Photo: David Neat

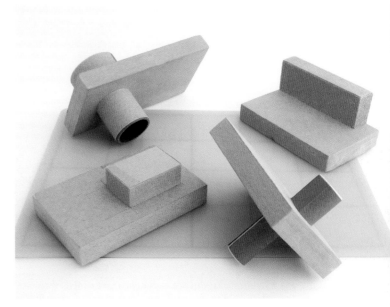

Customized sanding blocks made from MDF and PVC pipe. Inventing and making one's own simple tools according to need can save both time and effort.

For this window frame the basis was cut as one piece from PVC and fine, preformed styrene strip laid on it for the detailing of the struts and so on.

Windows cut into the PVC façade were smoothed using a sanding block like this.

Because styrene can be bent easily into curves it has been used on the house façade for the sides of the window openings. This photo on page 35 illustrates how the arched window was boxed in on the back face. A strip of styrene of the right length will keep to the curve when inserted into the box. All that it needs to secure it are spots of superglue around the outside. The round window next to it was first given a thickness of rigid foam to which the styrene was then glued. The special plastic solvent available to weld styrene (Plasticweld is a common brand) is so thin that it can be brushed from the outside, moving into the joint by capillary action and fusing it. This is useful, for example, in the case of a curved wall which needs to be secured in a particular shape before gluing (it would be impossible to apply glue to the edge first and then glue it down in the right place).

Styrene is not only useful in sheet form. A whole range of pre-formed strips, rods and tubes is also available. The decorative moulding on the façade was built up using some of these square or half-round section strips.

Working with foams

Two types of foam will be considered here. First are those which belong to the range of so-called 'rigid' foams (meaning that, although soft and light, the material will resist sufficiently to be easily cut, carved or sanded), including foamed polyurethane and polystyrene. Then there are those known under the brand name of Plastazote which are much more flexible and 'cushiony'.

Both are extremely useful for achieving a variety of forms, such as those which still require a largely constructional approach rather than fluid modelling but which would be very difficult or time-consuming to make using card or sheet plastic. They can be bought in sheet form just like the plastic, with shapes being cut out and assembled in much the same way. But in the case of rigid foam the material can then be broken down, sanded, carved into or even embossed with ease, which opens many more possibilities for creating shape or texture. Plastazote can't be sanded or carved in the same way, but its flexibility has other advantages.

Shown here is a collection of forms made almost entirely out of foam. Almost all have been built up in layers and then shaped. For some, a slightly harder material (PVC in these cases) has been added, either to provide support and strength or to function as formers while shaping. Different tools have been used to carve or impress, including a scalpel, fruit knife, wood files, wire brushes and sandpaper blocks.

A collection of forms that have been variously constructed, shaped, carved and sanded in foam.

Polystyrene

The pure white, ultra-light packing material most people know as polystyrene is the most familiar example of this foam. It should be referred to more properly, at least here in the UK, as expanded polystyrene because it's exactly the same material as the styrene featured previously. The only difference is that it has been 'popcorned' by being aerated under heat. It is a useful material for building up the basis of landscapes, if only because it can be had for free if one can bear to keep the unwieldy amounts of it that come with televisions and fridges. It can also be bought at specialist model shops in blocks and sheets of virtually any size. There is little need to say more because most people will be familiar with its coarse cellular structure and the fact that it is unsuitable for forms of any detail.

Styrofoam

This is a much more suitable and versatile material for model-making. To add to the confusion over names, styrofoam is the name given to the above white polystyrene in the USA. In the UK, it denotes the denser light-blue foam used to insulate walls and roofs, hence it's also known as blue foam, or Roofmate from an earlier brand name. It is the same type of polystyrene, although expanded in a different way, which gives it a much finer structure and the blue colour is just a dye added to differentiate it. There are other colours (pink, green and white, for example), each with a slightly different density. The white version is the finest and is significantly more expensive.

For most model-making purposes there's little to choose between them and so the cheaper blue variety is usually the best bet. This can be found in sheet form (commonly 25mm or 50mm thick) at builders' merchants or in specialized model shops in sheets (from 1mm upwards) or blocks of almost any size.

Gluing styrofoam is not entirely straightforward. A strong PVA (that is, a fast-acting wood glue rather than the 'school glue' variety) will work on small pieces if the surfaces are flush, but is not suitable for laminating large areas together. Solvent-based glues such as superglue, UHU or Evo-Stik contact adhesive will just dissolve the surface. UHU has developed a special alternative, UHU por, which will work if applied to both surfaces first. To bond large areas together, or to bond foam with plastic, double-sided tape can be most effective.

For the same reason that solvent-based glues will not work, some paints, notably spray paints, will eat into the surface of styrofoam because they often contain acetone as a base. In this event the surface would need to be thoroughly sealed with a water-based varnish or shellac. Painting with a thin layer of polyfilla, gesso or acrylic primer may not be sufficient because the acetone may soak through this layer onto the foam.

The destructive action of acetone on styrofoam can sometimes be used to good effect. In the unpainted rock examples shown here, the effect of acetone has been utilized to break down the surfaces in a particularly unpremeditated fashion, exposing the layers of polyfilla that have been used as a glue in this case. There is a method of 'lost foam' casting, in which the prototype is made from styrofoam and a soft plaster shell applied to it. Acetone can then be used to dissolve completely

This illustrates the method of combining a soft foam with another substance to produce a particular structural effect. In this case, a quick way of mimicking the form of layered rock was needed. Styrofoam was roughly cut into thinner strips and a block prepared (shown in the background), cementing the layers together with polyfilla. After this has completely set the block can be cut into shapes. The styrofoam can be easily broken down, but the harder Polyfilla layers resist and are accentuated. Acetone was used in this case to eat away the foam in a particular way while leaving the polyfilla.

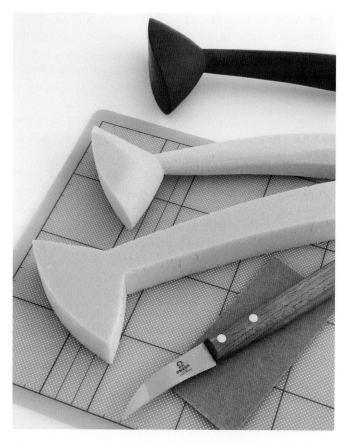

ABOVE: **To create this form the outline shape was cut in styrofoam, which was then carved with a knife, rasped or sandpapered to form a smooth, curved surface. The styrofoam can then be coated with Polyfilla and sanded before painting. The surface is delicate but sufficient for light handling.**

BELOW: **Sample constructions showing Kapa-line foamboard used in the more conventional way. The piece at the bottom shows an invisible join and top left illustrates how the foamboard can be made to bend smoothly by removing the paper on one side.**

the prototype and a harder plaster can be cast into the hollow shell. The softer plaster layer can now be chipped away, exposing the cast.

Polyurethane foam

The majority of the examples illustrated here were made from a slightly different type of rigid foam that forms the main constituent of Kapa-line foamboard made by the German firm Alcan Kapa. This board was never intended for this kind of use. Kapa-line is just a superior form of foamboard produced in the usual thicknesses (3.5mm, 5mm and 10mm), the main difference being that the foam inside is polyurethane rather than the weaker polystyrene. Because of this, the foam forms a different bond with the paper covering and this can be carefully peeled off either from one or both sides, leaving the foam relatively intact. What one is left with is a thin sheet of a good quality, fine-grained and amazingly versatile material.

Even if used only (as intended) as a straight foamboard, Kapa-line will offer many advantages. Because the foam inside has its own integrity and will carve or sand well, it is possible to make clean, precise chamfered (angled) edges. Being polyurethane, a range of glues can be used to bond it, enabling much stronger and cleaner construction. In fact, the foam edge is dense enough to allow bonding with thin strips of double-sided tape, which means that models can be dismantled if need be relatively easily. The photo illustrates these qualities, including the fact that the thinner versions of Kapa-line can be bent into soft curves just by removing the paper from one side. For tighter curves, it may need assistance by lightly scoring the exposed foam and controlling the area where it can bend. If this is not enough, slivers of foam can be removed along these lines or deeper grooves sanded with a nail file.

Also illustrated is a common technique used by those who prefer to make clean presentational models out of foamboard. When two pieces are joined to form a right angle, the foam can be carefully cut and sanded away at the end of one piece to form a lip of paper which hides the foamboard edge of the other piece.

Building forms in sections and layers

If specific, controlled shapes are needed, the polyurethane foam may not be sufficient on its own because it offers too little resistance to sanding. It is too easy to go too far. In these cases, the foam needs to be combined with templates, or stops made from a more resilient material in order to control the formation of the shape.

The 'snowman' shape with its constructional drawing.

polyurethane foam used in Kapa-line foamboard is exceptionally flexible for these purposes. Thin strips can be bent into quite tight curves or even twisted without breaking. Other types of polyurethane foam sheet are available (without paper covering), but these tend to be the more rigid, brittle variety.

Fluted columns can be easily made by sanding grooves into a piece of foam while still flat and then wrapping them around a tube support. The grooves will help the foam to bend. In the examples shown here the bases are built up from circles of foam, variously shaped to create an interesting profile. Some of these have been combined with circles of PVC to keep the shape regular. For the more complex 'sugar-twist' form, strips of foam were first sanded round on one side and then wrapped around the tube support. In cases where the foam is under tension, double-sided tape will not be strong enough, it is better to use a contact adhesive such as Evo-Stik Impact. Although this type of glue will dissolve styrofoam, it will work perfectly well on polyurethane.

In the above example a regular 'snowman' shape was built up in sections of foam with PVC formers in-between to serve as stops when the foam is sanded down. Double-sided tape formed a strong enough bond between foam and plastic. The shape needed to be drawn first in profile and divided into sections corresponding to the thickness of foam used, allowing also for the PVC dividers. A flat sanding block was used to ensure that the foam was not sanded beyond the extent of these dividers.

For this next example, a fragment of church window, the subject was first drawn to establish the outside line and the inside limit for the chamfer on the masonry. These two templates were then photocopied, spray-mounted onto 1mm PVC and cut out. Foam was then also spray-mounted onto the larger silhouette and cut out, using it as a guide for the blade. The outside edge was roughly squared, sanding with a nail file in this case, and the inner shape was glued in the right position. The chamfer can then be carved or sanded using these two extents as guides. The outer profile was made by sanding an edge of the foam sheet with a round file, cutting this edge off as a thin strip and curving and gluing into place. The particular

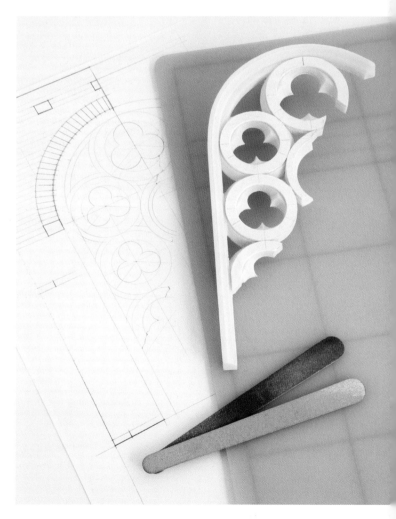

This form was made by sandwiching foam between two harder PVC templates and sanding down the edge of foam in-between.

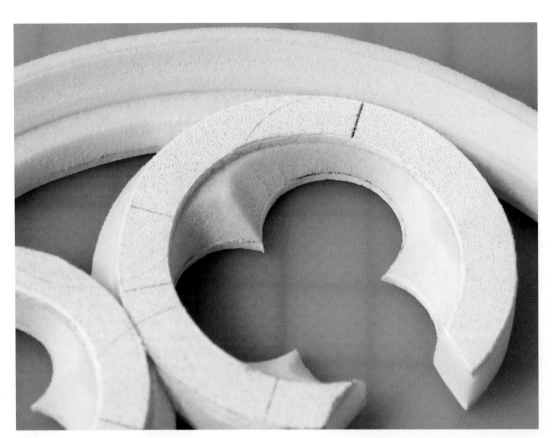

Detail showing chamfered edges.

BELOW: Column shapes assembled from pieces of foam. The fluting was achieved by running a round file along the foam surface.

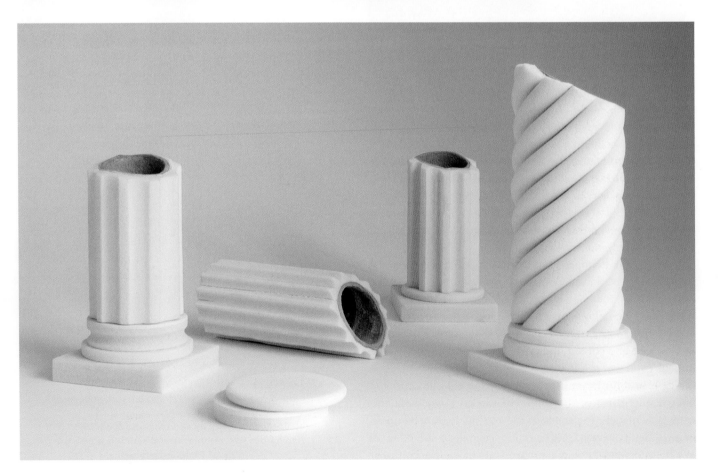

Using flexible
Plastazote to build
up a profile round a
curved surface. Once in
place the material
can be primed and
painted with acrylic.
A rubber-based contact
adhesive is the best
type of glue to use.

Plastazote

This is a flexible sheet foam, similar to cushion foam but usually much denser. The unusual name originates as a brand name from a company called Zotefoams. All manner of densities, hardnesses, thicknesses and colours are produced. It is used extensively in bespoke packaging of costly items and in healthcare for supports and splints. The thicker, industrial versions are very popular with puppet-makers because it enables the making of a strong, yet flexible, lightweight shell. Thinner, softer and more colourful sheets have found their way into hobby shops. Its full and correct description is 'low-density, closed-cell, cross-linked polyethylene foam'! Like other foams (expanded polystyrene, styrofoam and so on) it is composed of cells, which can vary in size with different types, from fine (0.2mm) to large cell (1mm).

Because it can be cut very easily and cleanly, while also being very flexible and moderately elastic, it is ideal for constructing more organic curved shapes, and for applying strips (for mouldings) to curved surfaces. For example, it's useful where a profile is needed around the base of a column, as illustrated here. Although it remains spongy, the surface is relatively tight, so, if primed with acrylic, it can be painted to resemble stone or any material you choose. It is too flexible to properly carve or sand and will accept only certain glues. Superglue will work with many, especially the finer, softer ones. The recommended type of glue for all types is synthetic rubber contact adhesive, for example Evo-Stik Multi-Purpose Impact. This is applied to both surfaces and allowed to dry until it has almost lost its 'stick'. Then the two surfaces are pressed firmly together. The bond can be pretty strong, even edge to edge. Plastazote can also be moulded to a small extent, in that it can be pulled out of shape, especially when subjected to a little heat.

HEALTH AND SAFETY

Some care must be taken while using any of these materials, including those that might seem perfectly harmless. For example, polyurethane dust can be an irritant because it is abrasive and a dust mask should be worn while sanding. Good ventilation is essential when using any solvents or solvent-based glues, particularly superglue and contact adhesive. It is also just as important to consider posture while working, particularly since model-making can involve long hours hunched over something small. Regular 'stretching breaks' should be taken and ideally your work chair should be set significantly lower than normal.

CHAPTER 3

METHODS OF CASTING

Introduction

This chapter puts forward a very simplistic account of casting for those who may have done little of it. It addresses the main questions first. Why and when should one consider casting? What are the basic methods? Which are the least complicated materials and where can they be found? More importantly, for those who have yet to discover the possibilities, it illustrates the fact that casting may be an option for forms one wouldn't otherwise consider. What follows is a quick overview, before we consider example cases in detail.

When is casting necessary or useful?

Obviously having the means to reproduce a form relatively quickly is a blessing if you need to make more than ten of them. Some forms lend themselves to casting more readily than others – a beer keg, for example, as opposed to a chandelier. But it is surprising what forms can be achievable with just a little extra effort and, as you will see, even the chandelier could become a candidate for casting with a little more skill and ingenuity.

Casting is useful not only for the repetition of individual forms such as beer kegs, but for individual parts which can be repeated and then assembled into a larger or more complex form. An example might be the ornamental strip illustrated. Here, the prototype has been made for one unit which can then be repeated to form a continuous strip. (The word 'prototype' will be used throughout this chapter to describe the initial form, because obviously 'model' may become confusing.) The detail is complex so the time invested in getting the prototype right and in making a mould of it would be a fraction of the time and concentration needed to sculpt units individually. Better than that, the silicone mould used in this case will keep for many years if properly looked after, to be used over again. Since the form is a component, it could be combined with others to contribute to different forms if needed. For example, if corner pieces are made these could be put together to make a complete frame.

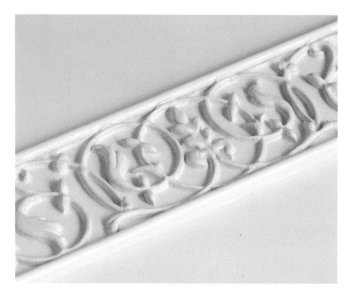

ABOVE: **The prototype for an ornamental strip. The basis of the pattern has been carefully cut out of foamed PVC to form a raised template onto which relief paint (*see* Chapter 5) has been piped to round off the effect.**

BELOW: **The completed mould together with castings.**

These chairs have been cast in separate pieces and then assembled.

Illustrating the casting process. Objects of this detail and delicacy require a relatively robust silicone for the mould and a fluid resin for the casts. These were cast in two-part polyurethane resin and the silicone used was a pouring one with a fairly high Shore A hardness of 55.

Transforming a material (from the series *Excavations* by Astrid Bärndal and Marc Steinmetz).

Thinking in this way (of components which can be variously assembled) leads one to realize that many things can be accomplished quite easily. An example of this would be the 1:25 chair illustrated. In itself it is a delicate, involved form which one would never imagine being able to cast while thinking about it in one piece! But divided into three components – back, seat and front legs – it becomes relatively straightforward.

Sometimes it's necessary (or particularly prudent) to develop a form as a cast if you need to experiment with the finish. It may be a little more time-consuming than creating a one-off, but it certainly alleviates the tension if you're not sure whether your treatment will work or if you want to try a variety of alternatives.

Casting also becomes essential if you have to transpose a prototype from one material to another, as in the case of producing a durable plaster version of a plasticine form. In this case, it may only be one casting which is needed but it is still an advantage to be able to make more.

The basics

The first thing to come to terms with is that everything in casting is interdependent and that it is not a process that can be rushed into without having a definite plan for each stage. The nature of the form to be reproduced will determine the choice of mould-making material, the type of mould (that is, whether it needs just one part or many) and the material it can be cast in. On the other hand (and working backwards), the use to which the cast is to be put (that is, whether this will be glued, painted or worked into and how long it is supposed to last) will equally determine the choice of casting material, affecting the method of casting and the design of the prototype.

The prototype

In a sense, the prototype can be made out of anything that will maintain its shape long enough for a moulding material to cover it and set. Every surface detail of the prototype is transferred to the mould in this process and if the mould endures the prototype will no longer be needed. Fossils are the most beautiful and poignant illustration of this. They are nature's way of telling us that negatives can form the templates for new creation. Nature is also telling us, by the way, how easy it can be to make casts! No particular skill was needed for dinosaur footprints to reach us perfectly preserved after millions of years, only the right materials and conditions. Early humankind made use of similar inspiration and the technique of sand casting is still practised today. For this, an exact impression of a form is made in sand (which is usually bound together with oil) and metal is cast directly into it.

Undercutting

You will need to be able get the hardened cast out of the mould as easily as possible if you wish to use the mould repeatedly. Moulds made in flexible materials will assist in this and that's what they're designed for, but there will be a limit to how much they will flex. If you fill a balloon with plaster and let it set, the rubber will only stretch so far to allow you to take the plaster out – the bulb is far bigger than the stalk. Undercutting is the word used to describe this difference and it applies not only to the overall shape but to every surface detail. This doesn't mean that the form has to be simplified until there is no more undercutting – the form is the last thing that should be compromised – but it does mean that the method of making the mould has to adapt. Perhaps the object needs to be cast in two parts, involving two separate moulds. Or it is more usual to pour the cast in one, but make the mould in more than one part which can then be easily removed from the cast object.

ABOVE: **Another prototype unit for a decorative frieze being made, this time at a larger scale. The fragile Kapa-line foam used for the details needs only to be sealed and to withstand the silicone rubber being poured over it for the form to become more permanent. Prototypes can combine any variety of materials as long as they will temporarily hold together. Photo: David Neat**

BELOW: **The result cast in white concrete. Photo: David Neat**

Access

It must also be made as easy as possible for the casting material (usually liquid at first) to fill every bit of the mould. This is simplest in the case of a flat object where the mould becomes a simple tray that just needs to be poured to the brim. Having this access means that air which might become trapped between mould and liquid will have an easy escape and be assisted to the surface. But for a form that is to be seen from all sides, such as a figure, there are hardly any blank or flat areas that can be used as openings from which to pour. It is usually done through the feet, but this means that one has to pour through the smallest of openings. More crucially, it means that the only escape for the air coming out can become blocked by the casting material going in. The way this problem is usually solved is by cutting small channels at various points deeper in the mould so that air can escape out of them. These will inevitably fill with casting material once the air is forced out and will become an unwanted part of the cast, but it will be easy enough to remove them. The other precaution is to build up the area around the feet, perhaps even filling the space between the legs, for better access. These extras can be similarly removed from the cast once it can be worked on.

Mould release

One has to be sure that the mould can be easily and cleanly parted from the prototype once it is set and the same applies between the mould and the cast. Most mould-making materials will be fairly non-stick anyway, but some precautions still have to be made. The surface of the prototype needs to be made as non-absorbent as possible. When this is a dense modelling material such as plasticine it is not a problem, but if other materials such as wood, plaster or foam are used the surface will have to be thoroughly sealed. Various undercoats or varnishes could be used to seal the surface of wood or plaster, but some may react with mould-making materials such as silicone or polyurethane rubber. Some may also start dissolving the surface of styrofoam. If in doubt, it's best to stick with a sealer that will be safe in any event such as the simplest water-based acrylic undercoat. The surface of the prototype doesn't have to be hard, just impervious. Another form of sealant that is always safe to use is shellac, which is a natural preparation made from the resinous secretion of a particular insect dissolved in alcohol.

A further barrier may be needed even after sealing the surface of the prototype to serve more as a lubricant assisting the release from the mould. The most common to use is a petroleum jelly such as vaseline. Only a very thin coating is necessary, otherwise it might clog fine detail on the prototype. The directions which come with the different mould-making compounds advise the use of different release agents and on the whole this advice should be trusted. There is usually less need for a release agent between the finished mould and the cast, except in the case of a plaster mould, but using one anyway can often result in better castings and lengthen the life of the mould.

Common mould-making materials

The various materials which can be used for moulds are not interchangeable, that is, what one might achieve another won't. Although some common properties are shared there are fundamental differences. Some, such as latex, can only be used to make a skin mould (they have to be brushed on in layers), whereas others need to be poured into a block. Some are suitable for both brushing on or pouring, usually with the aid of special additives. The types are listed below.

Latex

This may be the simplest means of making some forms of mould; indeed, it can be so simple that children are encouraged to try it, by covering some basic form such as a plaster gnome figure with successive layers of latex, rolling it off when

dry and filling the shape with plaster. This can work for forms which are very limited in shape and where distortions aren't much of a problem. Latex shrinks, unlike the other materials listed here, and there is a limit to the thickness that can be built up before the surface becomes lumpy. It cannot be poured as a block. It starts as a milky liquid and dries by evaporation, becoming a translucent beige. Because it can be layered to form flexible skins it is ideal for a particular form of casting illustrated at the end of this chapter which is useful for reproducing surface effects. Here it serves, not as the mould-making substance, but as the material for the casts.

Silicone rubbers

Silicone rubbers are by far the most commonly used in various disciplines where good-quality casting is required. They are essential if very fine surface detail needs to be reproduced. They are supplied in liquid form accompanied by a hardening (or more properly 'curing') ingredient, the catalyst. A measured amount of this catalyst needs to be thoroughly mixed with the rubber before pouring. After that, the rubber will take anything from two hours to one day to harden, depending on the type of rubber used. The different types will have different degrees of hardness, meaning that some will flex well to accommodate undercuts while others will not. They are expensive, averaging about £25 for a litre, but for small-scale work this amount can go a long way. Unfortunately, they generally have a 'shelf life' (the amount of time they can be kept before being used) of six to twelve months, which is a disadvantage if they are used only occasionally.

Polyurethane rubbers

These have much the same properties as silicone and there is also a range of different types. There may be little to choose between polyurethane and silicone, but some polyurethanes work out cheaper. Another difference is that usually they come in two equal parts to be mixed 1:1, which makes mixing a bit simpler. Using silicone may be safer though, especially if you intend to cast in polyurethane resin, because although this resin will work in a polyurethane mould if it is properly coated first, mishaps can occur.

Gelflex

If money is a problem there is Gelflex. This is a re-meltable vinyl which comes in a block very similar to jelly and has almost the same feel. It must be melted first to make it liquid and pourable. Its advantages are that it is a lot cheaper than silicone and that it can also be used more than once. Moulds which are no longer needed can be cleaned up, chopped and re-melted. Gelflex also has a much longer shelf life than silicone, in fact almost indefinite. It comes in a choice of two hardnesses, though even the hard version is quite soft compared to the harder silicones available. The disadvantage is that Gelflex needs to be melted at a temperature of around 150°C and poured soon after. A plastic, foam or plasticine prototype would melt or distort, so the initial form-making is limited to using such materials as wood, plaster or polymer clay. Vinamold is another brand almost identical to Gelflex.

Plaster

Plaster can be used both as a casting and a mould-making material under special circumstances. Its disadvantage for making moulds is that it is not flexible, which means that it can either only be used for very simple forms involving no undercutting whatsoever, or that it has to be built up as a shell which can be parted in sections. A third alternative is possible if used with a casting material which is in itself flexible, as is the case when casting latex skins into a plaster negative. Plaster is relatively cheap and available, but the standard type sold in building supply centres that is used for plastering walls is not suitable for these purposes. It is usually either too coarse, too soft or takes too long to set. Either plaster of Paris (still available from some chemists and DIY centres), or an especially hard casting plaster are much better for this and can be obtained from sculpture supply shops. Before it can be used as a mould the plaster must be fully dried and sealed with shellac or water-resistant PVA.

Using found objects as moulds

Although not illustrated, it may be worth considering the 'opportunist' approach of using found forms such as ice-making trays or plastic packaging shapes to cast in. This relies either on having a good memory for these possibilities or keeping a stock of them around. Ready-made moulds of various shapes can also be found in some hobby or sculpture shops for making clear resin castings.

Common casting materials

Polyurethane resin

Polyurethane resin has been used for most of the following

examples. It comes in two liquid parts that have to be mixed thoroughly in equal amounts (1:1) and then poured. The type used here will stay transparent until it starts to set, after which it will become increasingly opaque. This transparency is an advantage because there should be just enough time to see any air bubbles which might have become trapped in the mixture when pouring into a simple flat mould. These can be teased to the surface with a piece of wire. Setting is fast, however, and casts can usually be removed from the mould after fifteen minutes. They may still be slightly flexible, but this can also be an advantage in getting them out of the mould and trimming off any unwanted parts at this 'green' (a term borrowed from woodwork) stage. If bent in this way, a flat cast should be bent back and laid flat to continue hardening. It may be anything from a few hours to a few days before hardening is completed.

Plaster

This is by far the cheapest material for making casts and it can have a lot of strength, although it will be far too brittle to make the examples illustrated so far. Plaster of Paris (or better still a fine casting plaster such as Basic Alpha) will flow well and reproduce a lot of detail. Dependent upon the type, plaster will set quickly and can be taken out of the mould in as little as twenty minutes. It is perfect for beer kegs (even minute ones), rocks, simple figures or anything which has a similarly robust form. Plasters are mixed by shaking them into water until almost all the water appears to have been filled, then stirring thoroughly. They will seem thick and sluggish when first mixed but flow better when agitated, so getting them into even small mould openings is not as hard as first appears if the mould is shaken or tapped while doing it.

Super Sculpey

The polymer clay Super Sculpey (a particular type from the Sculpey range) features, like Kapa-line foamboard, in just about every chapter of this book because it is so versatile. It has been used to make some of the prototypes in this chapter, but it can also be used as a press-casting material if the mould will allow it. Because it becomes very malleable without being sticky it can be pressed and squeezed into quite deep shapes moulded in plaster or hard silicone and eased out while still soft without too much damage to the shape. If this is difficult the clay can be heated while still in the mould to harden it, either by blasting it for a while with a heat gun or putting it and the mould in the oven at a low setting. A plaster mould will survive this and so will silicone rubber if it's one of those designed to withstand soft metal casting, which the harder ones usually are.

Example 1: casting a chair using silicone rubber and resin

Because the components of the chair are very small, slender and with fine surface detail, only a good-quality silicone rubber will serve for the mould and only a resin will have the necessary strength when cast. The forms composing this chair are flat without any undercutting and the mould has to be stable to keep them in shape, so a relatively hard silicone was chosen. Silicones are differentiated by their Shore A hardness, the one here being 55 (the relative hardness of elastic materials such as rubber, soft plastics or silicone is determined by using an instrument called a Shore A durometer, which establishes the hardness of a material by the degree to which the durometer can pierce the material, which is then judged from 0 to 100). Softer silicones, which will flex to allow more undercutting, may be as little as 10 on the scale. The other reason for a hard silicone in this case is that excess resin will be wiped from the surface using the edge of a scraper and it needs to stay flat for this.

The process

The chair was first fully drawn up, with frontal, side and overhead views. Making the parts followed much the same layering process as described in Chapter 2, 'Constructing'.

1. A flat material such as smooth card or PVC is chosen as a base. The chair components are then built up on it, in this case a first layer of 1mm PVC cut-outs, which are then clad with obeche wood, bringing them up to an appropriate scale thickness. Superglue has been used as an adhesive. Remember that casting will unify all materials into one, so it doesn't matter what mixture of materials one starts with. The components can be kept quite close but, of course, not touching. Since silicone is expensive it makes sense to keep moulds to the minimum size possible. Obeche has been used to give the chairs a realistic sense of grain and this has been enhanced in places by scraping with coarse sandpaper. The silicone will pick up the fine detail of the wood grain and transfer this to the resin.

2. It is very important, particularly with silicone, that all the components are secured flat on the base and that any gaps are sealed. Although silicone will appear to be a thick, sluggish liquid and quite the opposite of water, it will work its way into the finest of cracks before it sets. This property makes it ideal for reproducing fine detail, but it means you have to be stringent in containing it. The coat of vaseline will block it from creeping underneath in this case, but for any larger gaps a surer way is to fill with plasticine. The excess has to be scraped or smoothed away.

3. Vaseline (which can be found in any chemist) must be used as a sealant, otherwise the silicone would stick to the wooden parts. Not all prototypes need to be sealed when

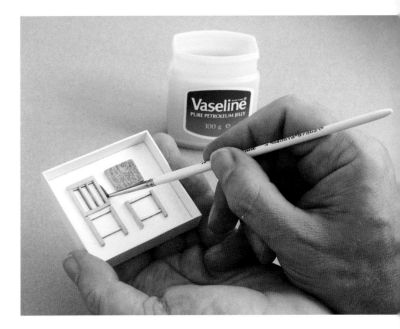

ABOVE: **Brushing a thin barrier of vaseline on the prototype.**

LEFT: **The prototype chair pieces stuck to a base of PVC.**

using silicone or Gelflex, but it's necessary if the materials are porous. The coating should be as thin as possible otherwise the whole effect of the grain might be lost. A fine brush has been used in this case.

4. As already seen, a temporary wall has to be built around the forms to contain the silicone. In this case, these walls are strips of PVC attached with superglue. Cardboard and PVA would work just as well for something of this size if the base is also cardboard. Another method, which can be even quicker and more entertaining, is to use Lego bricks. The silicone won't stick to them, they're reusable, strong enough to withstand the weight with larger moulds and the corners are tightly sealed. It helps if the wall construction is tacked to the baseboard with small portions of double-sided tape or with strips of masking tape around the outside to keep it in place. Vaseline should also be smeared along the inside edge. The mould wall should obviously be built up to a level above the highest point of your prototype. It is best to allow at least 5mm extra when using a hard silicone, but 10mm for a soft one.

5. The moment has now come to mix the silicone. The type used here is called RTV 101 and was supplied by the specialist sculpture outlet, Tiranti. This can be a moment of slight anxiety at first, not being sure how things will turn out and not wishing to waste an expensive material, but if all the steps are covered there's not a lot that can go wrong. The catalyst has to be dosed into the silicone as directed by the product information, but there is often quite a bit of leeway. Nowadays catalysts for silicone are usually supplied in dropper bottles and the directions are very clear as to how many drops are needed per 100ml of silicone (there is no need to dose by weight). In this case, the tin states that between eight to sixteen drops are needed per 100g of silicone (1g in weight will approximate 1ml in volume). It is advisable to aim for the middle. Less will mean a slightly longer 'pot life' (meaning the amount of time one has to work before the product starts setting) and often a longer overall setting time. More will have the opposite effect. The worst that could happen is that by adding too much catalyst each time you might run out of it.

You will need a calibrated beaker to measure the amount of silicone (available from suppliers of silicones or from craft shops). It is not a good idea to tip the can and pour the silicone into the beaker because this will lead to a mess. Using a large spoon and ladling the silicone like honey is preferable. This type of silicone has a long pot life so taking the time to make sure both components are thoroughly mixed is not a problem. Because the mixture can be quite viscous a strong spoon or thick wooden stick is needed. When mixing any form of synthetic compound it's important that these are clean, because chemicals such as paint or varnish remaining from their last use could affect the curing process. Estimating how much silicone is needed to fill a particular area is simple. 1ml of the liquid will occupy 1 cubic centimetre space, so, for example, if the mould measures 10 × 10cm and has to be filled to a height of 1cm, 100ml of silicone is needed. The size of the prototype taking up space within that is minimal in this case and will not make much of a difference.

ABOVE: **Lego used to make a mould wall. This doesn't need to be stuck to the base as long as it's perfectly flat; securing with masking tape around the outside should suffice.**

RIGHT: **Preparing to make a mould, showing a tin of silicone with the catalyst, measuring beaker, mixing sticks, spoon and prepared prototype.**

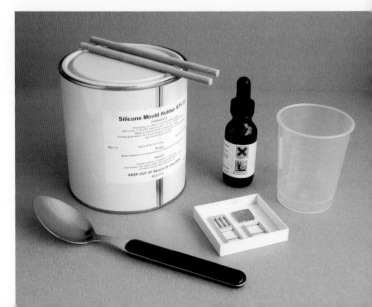

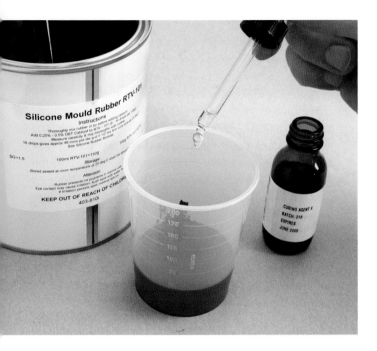

Adding catalyst to a measured amount of silicone.

could take the precaution of pouring just enough in to coat the form and leaving it for five minutes before pouring in the rest. Unless the deadline is tight, it's always best to choose a silicone with a long curing time. When the mould is filled to the appropriate level, leave it overnight and it should be ready in the morning. When the surface is completely dry to the touch, it is usually ready for 'demoulding'. A word of caution is necessary here though. At times, for whatever reason, the exposed surface of the silicone may be hard while the underneath parts may still be curing. This shouldn't normally happen, but it does occur from time to time. The mould walls should be dismantled and separated from the silicone block very carefully at first to check this. If the sides of the exposed block seem a lot softer than the top, the set-up should be left, preferably for another day, before separating the mould from the prototype.

6. There is no right or wrong way to pour silicone rubber (that is, whether one should pour from the centre outwards or otherwise), because it will remain a liquid for maybe a few hours and that will be ample time for any trapped air bubbles to rise to the surface. However, one

7. The whole mould wall can now be dismantled and the silicone block eased off the prototype. Building this on a plastic base will have helped because this will flex to ease the parting. It is worth trying to preserve the prototype just in case another mould has to be made from it – if many duplicates need to be cast, having two or three moulds to use at once will obviously make the task much quicker.

8. Before filling with resin, the interior of the mould can be lightly brushed with vaseline. This is not strictly necessary between silicone and polyurethane resin, but it does help

Pouring the mixture onto the prototype.

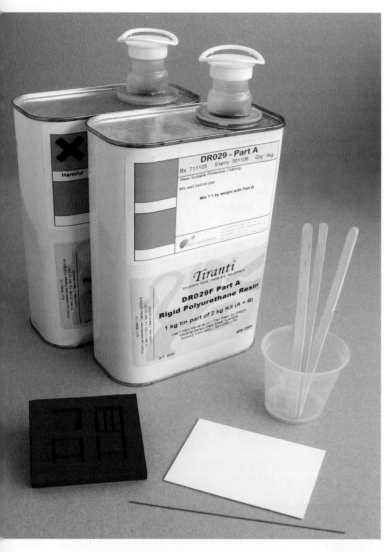

ABOVE: **Preparing for casting, showing two-part polyurethane resin, a clean calibrated beaker and mixing sticks, mould, plastic scraper and wire.**

BELOW: **The two resin parts are slightly different in colour, helping one to judge when they are mixed.**

to make the mould last longer. Minute fragments of silicone will come away with each casting, making the mould more ragged each time. Using vaseline, or an appropriate mould release agent, can help to minimize this. It should be used very thinly to preserve the surface detail.

The resin can now be mixed. As before, use a small calibrated beaker, dosing out first a small measure of one part followed by an equal measure of the other. The parts of this chair will need only a miniscule amount, so mixing too much is unavoidable. It is always a good idea to think of another use for the excess, such as another larger mould if you have it. Mixing has to be done quickly because you may only have a few minutes to pour it before it starts to thicken. As before, always use something clean for this. Usually the two parts of the resin will have a slightly different colour and consistency, so stir just as long as is necessary for the mixture to become one clear colour (perhaps stirring for a few more seconds for good measure).

Next, drip just enough of the resin onto the mould so that it covers the forms, then, using the wire (or a cocktail stick), make sure that it has filled every part. Look for air bubbles which might be trapped in tight corners and tease them out. Then, just as quickly, take a smooth edge of plastic or metal and run it along the flat of the mould with just a little pressure. This should push excess resin to the side, leaving the parts to be cast filled only to the lip. The parts of the chair will therefore come out suitably flat and can be sanded if necessary.

9. The resin used here is DRO 29 and is also supplied by Tiranti. This type starts clear, as we have seen (which is an advantage for locating air bubbles), but it sets off-white. As the resin starts to set, milky streaks will appear and from this point it will no longer be workable. Resin sets by means of a chemical reaction between the two parts and this generates heat. This will hardly be noticeable when mixing very small amounts, but the more resin mixed the hotter the mixture becomes. This also means that larger amounts of resin will start to harden at a quicker rate because the heat generated will accelerate the setting. If casting something like a block, the middle will set very quickly because the heat is concentrated there, while the edges will remain liquid. It may appear at first as if something has gone wrong, but one just needs to wait until each part has set. A good indication to scrape the thin film of resin that may have been left on the mould surface. If this is no longer tacky and can be peeled off almost as a skin, the other parts are ready to be removed.

10. One can choose to take a resin cast out of the mould while parts of it are still a bit rubbery, or it can be left there until the whole is more rigid. The advantage of the first

ABOVE: **Excess resin is cleanly scraped away before setting starts.**

LEFT: **Air bubbles are quickly teased out using a piece of wire.**

The chair components cast, trimmed and being assembled.

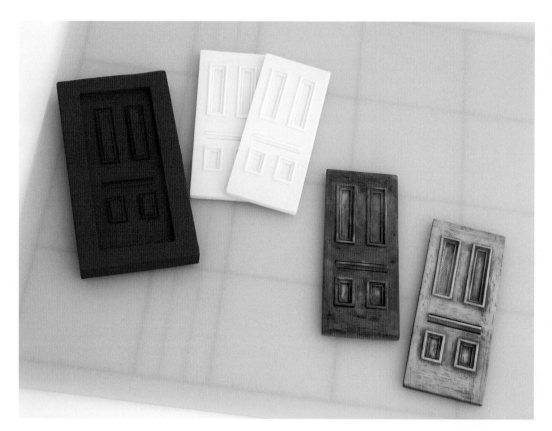

Another example – casting panelled doors, showing the mould, castings and painted examples.

approach is that unwanted edges are much easier to trim in this 'green' state before full hardening is completed. The pieces will bend as you prise them out, but the plastic already has a 'memory', meaning that the pieces are likely to straighten themselves out again if left flat. If, for example, you intend to use a flat casting, such as the ornamental strip to wrap round a column shape, this should be done while the plastic is still in this flexible state. Double-sided tape will hold the piece in place and it can be bound with masking tape for good measure. This will have to be left for at least a few days before the resin has totally set in this position.

11. The line of completed chairs featured at the start were painted with matt Humbrol enamel (specially formulated for painting on plastic) and then either given a dark wash or skimmed with coloured pencil to emphasize the grain. Acrylic will also usually work.

Example 2: casting rocks using Gelflex and plaster

The rock formation shown here is a more solid, robust form. Although silicone rubber and polyurethane resin would still be good choices for reproducing it, there are cheaper and quicker alternatives. Again, for this type of form only a simple one-part mould is needed, so the process will be very similar as for the previous example but the materials will be different.

Super Sculpey is the ideal choice for making the prototype for forms like this one which are rounded and have to be modelled rather than constructed. It is meant for baking in a domestic oven at around 130°C so it will withstand the hot Gelflex, hardening in the process. It is better though to harden it a little first before the mould is poured and to brush very lightly with vaseline to ensure that the Gelflex doesn't stick to the polymer clay. More information on working with Sculpey can be found in Chapter 5, 'Modelling'.

Because the form to be reproduced here has no slender parts, plaster can be used to make the casts. Standard plaster of Paris would just about be strong enough, but I have chosen a much harder, finer casting plaster. Although it costs a little more it is still a lot cheaper than using resin.

The process

1. The form has been modelled in Super Sculpey on a ceramic tile. The methods for modelling it are explained in more detail in Chapter 5, 'Modelling'. A tile has been used in this case because a base of cardboard or plastic would buckle with the heat.

Sealing the bottom edge of the Sculpey form ready for moulding.

Hardening the surface using a heat gun.

2. When ready, the form has to be heated a little to harden it and the simplest way is to use a heat gun. This tool is similar to a hairdryer but a great deal hotter. The gun should be kept in motion over the work, no closer than about 10cm, for about half a minute for something of this size. The reason is just to make the surface a little tougher, not to bake the whole thing through, so it shouldn't need very long. The alternative if you haven't got a heat gun is to use a domestic oven, as directed on the product. Both form and tile are put in the centre of a preheated oven for about ten minutes. If, after removing from the oven and cooling, the Sculpey form detaches itself from the tile it should be tacked down again with double-sided tape. As little air as possible should be trapped underneath the form, because this will expand under the hot Gelflex and pepper the mould with air bubbles as it cools. For this reason, the edge of the form was sealed again with fresh Sculpey. This small amount doesn't need to be hardened. Care was taken to remove any excess and to make the seal as smooth as possible.

3. A film of vaseline can then be brushed very lightly over the surface, trying not to obscure any finer details. This is a precaution, which is not always necessary because Gelflex will normally release itself from anything smooth, but it may help.

4. Gelflex will also need a mould wall to contain it and Lego can be used in the same way (see step 4 in Example 1). There will be some sticking of the Gelflex to the plastic because it slightly melts the surface but not enough to cause a problem.

5. The Gelflex can be heated up while doing this, but it needs to be watched and stirred constantly. Special heaters, similar to those used in batik for melting wax, are available but these are expensive instruments. With care, a normal saucepan can be used on a controllable heat source such as a small electric hotplate. A milk saucepan is ideal because it will have a pouring lip. Gelflex can be cut into smaller portions with a strong knife. It may seem logical to cut it into very small cubes to melt faster but this hardly makes a difference. What counts is the contact between

Covering with a thin coat of vaseline. A low wall of bricks at this point allows for easier access.

Gelflex being melted in the pan. This needs to be carefully watched and stirred constantly.

the Gelflex and the bottom of the saucepan. As it melts it should be moved around constantly, preferably with the other end of a wooden spoon. This type of blue Gelflex, which is the harder of two varieties, will turn slightly green when it overheats and this should be avoided by constant stirring. The pan should also be taken off the heat momentarily if this happens.

6. When the Gelflex is thoroughly liquid one should turn off the heat and wait for a little while, still stirring constantly, before pouring. This is because Gelflex will melt at 150°C but should be poured at 140°, as recommended in the directions for use. Pouring should be done quickly, which is different from the method used with silicone. This is because Gelflex will immediately start setting on contact with the cold prototype and will not work its way into detail in the same way as silicone. It is really only suitable for forms that have a minimum of surface detail or where absolute accuracy may not matter, as is the case here. In this case, the pouring was done in two stages, which proved effective. The first was to make sure that if any air was going to force itself from underneath (expanding with the heat), it would have a chance of escape. Gelflex can be poured in layers, the next melting and fusing with the previous if it is hot enough. Once the mould has cooled

(which may take an hour for a block of this size), it can be removed and made ready for the plaster.

7. First some water is put into a container. The rubber mixing cups sold in decorating shops make the best containers because the top can be squeezed together to make a spout when pouring. Instead of having to clean them afterwards, the remaining plaster can be left to dry and cracked off. It is always better to dispose of unused plaster like this anyway, because flushing wet plaster down the sink could eventually clog the pipes. Estimating the amount of water one should start with to reach the right amount of plaster needed is never easy, but one can usually assume that the volume will increase by about a third once the plaster is added. In this case a fine, hard casting plaster called Basic Alpha was used. It is always a good idea to sift the plaster first with a spoon to break up its compactness if it has been lying around for a while. The plaster can then be sprinkled steadily into the water, allowing it to absorb the water as it sinks. This should be continued until the water appears mostly filled with plaster, barring the top surface. It should then be thoroughly stirred until the mixture is even, knocking the pot a few times while doing this to help trapped air to escape. It is best to err on the thick side when mixing plaster rather than making it too thin.

Making the first
pour to surround
the form.

The mould can be
poured in stages.

Even if it appears at first too thick to pour it will loosen and flow better when agitated, whereas if it is too thin the cast could be quite weak. Stirring can provide a good indication. If you stir it with a little vigour and the mixture continues moving a little after you've stopped it is definitely too thin. Adding more plaster to a mix already stirred usually results in lumps and it may be better to start again. Incidentally, although the 'by eye' method is usually the simplest, most plasters come with directions stating the optimal plaster/water ratio if this fails to work.

After the plaster has been poured into the mould it should be tapped again to help air bubbles rise to the surface. Basic Alpha can be 'de-moulded' in as little as twenty minutes. The plaster will still be setting but will already be strong enough to be taken out.

Example 3: a two-part mould

So far, relatively simple forms have been considered which have included at least one flat side. Only simple one-part moulds were necessary for these. For the slightly more involved process of making a two-part mould for a form seen from both sides, there are a number of good books which can provide more detail, but the basics are outlined here.

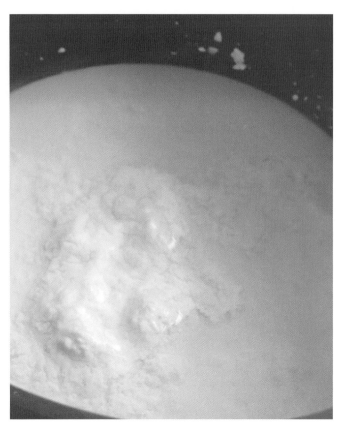

A good plaster/water ratio is usually obtained by continuing to sprinkle plaster into the water until the water appears almost filled.

The Gelflex mould together with unpainted castings.

Painted examples.

The process

1. This example features a small twisted branch form which needed to be cast and repeated. The prototype was made from styrene tube which had been heated and bent. The first stage in making the two-part mould involves embedding the prototype form halfway in plasticine. This will become the basis for the first mould half. The plasticine layer should follow the mid-point of the form as far as possible, with neither the half exposed nor the half embedded resulting in excessive undercuts. This is simple enough to achieve with a tubular shape in this case. The plasticine bed should be smoothed out. Finally for this stage, marks are depressed in the plasticine close to the form which will become the 'keying' marks in the silicone layer to come. The whole set-up is given a thin coating of vaseline.

2. It would be possible at this stage to press thin mould walls into the plasticine and cast a complete mould half in silicone. This may save time, but a cheaper method is to use a much thinner layer of silicone supported by a harder plaster 'jacket'. Most pourable silicones can be thickened with the addition of a special additive (a thixotropic agent), making them 'brushable'. Here silicone was brushed onto and around the form, building up a layer of about 5mm thick and extending at least 1cm around the form. Because the silicone in this state will no longer flow into all details of a form by itself, it needs to be carefully assisted with the brush. The silicone should also be brushed carefully into the depressions made in the plasticine for keying the two mould halves. It should be remembered that one end of the form needs to be left free to form the pouring end for the final castings.

A more complex 3-D form is embedded in plasticine for the first stage of making a two-part mould

The wall of brass shim positioned around the silicone jacket, ready for the outer plaster layer to be poured into it. Note how the shim is positioned close against the end of the branch. This will become the pouring end.

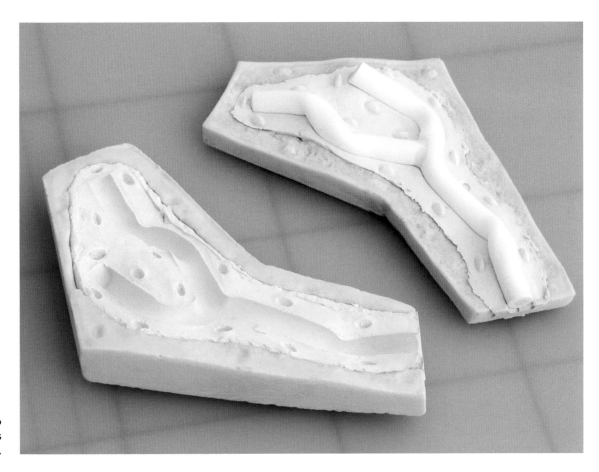

The two completed halves of the mould.

3. The silicone layer should be allowed to set fully; it is usually better to wait at least a day, depending upon the silicone type. A temporary wall can be pressed into the plasticine to hold the plaster. Here, thin brass shim was used (available from sculpture suppliers), but thin plastic or even cardboard could work just as well. After coating with vaseline, plaster can then be cast into this shape and allowed to set

4. After the plaster is dry, the shim walls can be taken off and all plasticine carefully removed from underneath. What's left is a complete mould half composed of a flexible silicone inner layer and a durable plaster outer jacket. The prototype must be left in, now embedded halfway in silicone. The whole process is repeated to make the second half of the mould directly onto this first half. The surface must be vaselined first, then silicone brushed over the

The completed forms assembled and ready for painting.

PRESS-MOULDING IN SUPER SCULPEY

Super Sculpey can serve very well in some simple cases as a casting material. If, for example, a mould for a very basic form is made from the heat-resistant RTV-101 (used for the chair previously), Sculpey can be pressed into the mould and baked to hardness while still there. The Sculpey should first be worked between the fingers to get it to maximum softness. It can then be pressed into the mould, working it around by repeatedly pressing and moving, to ensure that it has filled all detail. The excess, sitting proud of the flat mould surface, can easily be trimmed off with a scalpel blade and the top surface smoothed off. The mould is then put in the oven at 130°C for around fifteen minutes and left to cool completely before the hardened Sculpey form is taken out.

Another example shown here of the press-moulding method gives a slightly different application. This is for a sculptural assemblage rather than a strictly model one, but it serves to illustrate the method. A simple leaf shape was modelled in Sculpey and a Gelflex mould made, in the same way as for the rock form. Although the resultant Gelflex mould is much softer, Sculpey can still be pressed into it and smoothed off at the edges. By flexing the mould, the Sculpey can be detached and pulled carefully from it without much damage. This is an ideal method for reproducing a basic template shape which can then be modified. In this case, twisting or stretching the Sculpey will produce variations on the leaf form. These can then be placed on a heat-resistant surface such as a ceramic tile or baking tray and hardened in the oven.

exposed prototype half and its set silicone bed, keeping as far as possible to the same shape. The vaseline will stop the fresh silicone from fusing with the other half. When this silicone half is set, the plaster jacket can be cast over it. It may be easier to tack cardboard strips onto the existing plaster edges to form the casting walls. Again, this plaster must first be vaselined to prevent the second half from sticking to it.

Making latex skins

This is perhaps the very simplest form of casting and involving the least effort and expense. At times, it is useful to have a method of reproducing as much as you need of a specially patterned surface, such as roof tiles or cobblestones. All that is

**Press-moulding simple Sculpey shapes into a mould. These can then be twisted
or stretched to create variations before the Sculpey is baked.**

needed is a relatively dense surface on which the liquid latex can be spread. When dry, the latex can be peeled off as a continuous skin, having reproduced the texture or structure underneath. This will, of course, have been reproduced in negative form, but the results, when using a found surface as a base, can often be surprising. Latex will not stick to a non-porous surface, so no special release agent such as vaseline is needed. In fact, latex will not dry properly on vaseline so it should be avoided. Textured plastics, stone or any well-painted surface are ideal.

Latex will reproduce the grain of wood, although the wood surface, being absorbent, will need to be primed first. It is important to remember that latex will shrink, meaning that there will be a 5 to 10 per cent reduction in the size of the skin piece and of the pattern itself. The more layers used, the more shrinkage will occur.

Two methods are described here for specially creating moulds with a premeditated pattern. The first involves directly making the mould or negative in Kapa-line foam, sealing and

Moulds in Kapa-line foam at the bottom, with painted skin casts above.

filling it. For the second, a positive is first made in plasticine and a plaster cast is made from this, which can then be filled with the latex.

Making latex skin moulds from Kapa-line foam

As we have seen in the previous chapter (and will deal with again in Chapter 6, 'Creating Surfaces'), the foam within Kapa-line foamboard is very impressionable. A dimensional pat-

tern can easily be created by repeatedly pressing the end of a tool into it. If this surface is sealed (using acrylic primer, wall emulsion or gesso, for example), latex can be spread to fill the pattern and will peel off easily when dry. The photo here shows three small example moulds at the bottom with the painted latex casts made from them at the top. The tip of a jigsaw blade was used to create the fish-scale pattern on the right. The end of a small brush produced the cobblestone effect in the middle, while the end of a small metal ruler was used for the example on the left. These are intentionally small samples; working moulds could of course be much larger. It is best to experiment a little to see how deep a shape can be impressed in the foam before it starts to tear (these tear marks will be reproduced in the latex, but can be filled with polyfilla).

The mould surfaces will need a very slight lip around them to contain the latex, because it is easier to pour the liquid latex onto them rather than using a brush. Brushes will become immediately unusable as the latex begins to dry. A generous amount of latex can be poured on, moved around to fill the shape and then drained off. This will ensure a suitably thin and even coat. A good skin will usually need two coats, the process being repeated once the first coat is thoroughly dry. It is a good idea to add some base colouring to the latex mixture, as this will not only make the drying process and resulting cast easier to see, it will also make painting simpler. Colourings are available especially for latex, otherwise concentrated paint toners work just as well. Very little is needed to achieve a strong colour when dry, because the initial white in the latex will have disappeared. Latex is difficult to paint using water-based paints and the examples shown were dry-brushed using Humbrol enamel. This adheres very well to the surface and will also stretch with the latex. This is another advantage of creating a latex skin to cover a surface, the fact that the latex can be stretched or moulded around an uneven or curved support.

Creating a plaster mould

For the flint wall surface illustrated here a little more depth was required and the special shapes of the stones needed to be more individually modelled. A flat plasticine prototype was created on a PVC base and the plaster mould cast from it. Because the strong, quick-setting Basic Alpha plaster was used, the mould needed only to be about 1cm thick. Latex can be poured into the mould as soon as the plaster has set hard without the need for any other sealant. The other advantage of a plaster mould, apart from it lasting much longer, is that the first latex layer will set comparatively quickly because the plaster absorbs the water from it.

Plaster mould with latex casts. A little black has been added to the latex mixture.

Latex is spread by tilting the mould before the excess is poured off.

BELOW: A painted wall showing strips of the latex flint effect between other textures in Kapa-line foam.

A real flint wall for comparison. Photo: David Neat

CHAPTER 4

WORKING WITH METALS

Metals are not the easiest materials for the model-maker to use. Although there are various types with different qualities, most are problematic to cut, shape or join by simple means. Yet some knowledge of what can be done with certain types will be of great benefit for a variety of tasks and will be essential for some of them. What follows is not an all-embracing account of everything that can be achieved with metal. It is a selection based upon experience of what has proved to be most useful, effective or manageable in terms of budget and time. The general precept of this book, that there is little point in advocating materials which are difficult to find or skills which require a disproportionate amount of practice, applies here in particular.

Each part of this chapter consists of a generalized introduction to techniques, materials and equipment, followed by step-by-step accounts of the making of selected examples.

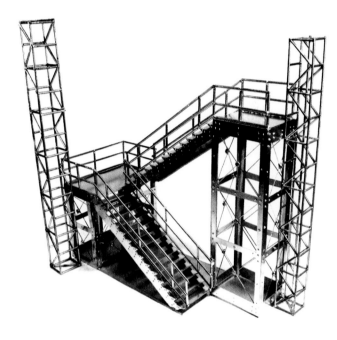

For this intricate 1:25 model of truss towers and steps, John P. Hall soldered the main construction in brass, adding steps, platforms and so on in thin card. Rivets were detailed using relief paint. The whole unit was then finished with chrome spray paint.

Soldering

Soldering involves applying enough localized heat to the two parts of metal meant to be joined so that a soft metal alloy known as solder will melt into the joint. When this has cooled it will form a firm, though still breakable, bond. Because the surface of metal oxidizes when hot, which would prevent the solder from bonding, a third substance known as flux needs to be applied beforehand to the joint area to prevent this. Soldering is simple and effective: as long as all these components are used; as long as the soldering iron can deliver sufficient heat for the task; and as long as it is the metal itself which is melting the solder. Those new to soldering will often assume that melting a little solder onto the tip of the iron and then smearing that over the joint will do the trick. The metal may appear to be stuck, but the bond will be weak because the metal itself hasn't been heated enough. The joint, apart from not lasting, will probably look rather messy (blobbed or encrusted), whereas if soldering is done properly the joint will be satisfyingly clean and invisible. This matters if you want to achieve the right look for anything slender or intricate, such as a brass bedstead or elegant balcony railings.

What equipment is needed?

Soldering irons come in different strengths, indicated by the wattage. An iron of between 12W and 20W will be suitable for spot-soldering fine electrical wires or circuit boards, but will not deliver enough heat to cope with 2mm brass rod. What distinguishes a stronger iron is not so much how hot it can get, but how much it can sustain that heat when it is drawn away by the metal. Thicker metal will draw the heat away quickly and a weak iron will struggle to maintain an optimum temperature. The iron would need to be rested, that is, taken away from the work to regain this temperature, but trying again will not make the metal any hotter. For most model-making purposes, a 30–40W iron is needed.

It is also better to buy an iron with a removable bit (the tip of the iron making contact with the work). Different shapes are usually available and a fine 'pencil' shaped bit, for example, may not be the best means of delivering heat to two adjoining pieces of metal at the same time. A broader 'screwdriver' shaped bit would be better for this. A great deal depends on the bit making as much contact as possible with the metal so that the heat can be transferred without interruption. For this reason, the bit needs to be kept clean during soldering. It will collect a layer of oxidization and spent flux, so wiping it regularly on a damp sponge is essential. Some soldering irons are sold with a small sponge pad for this purpose.

The most effective solder to use, at least for brass or copper, is a 60/40 tin/lead alloy (meaning 60 per cent tin to 40 per cent lead). This is the type one generally finds. There are other solders available, for example one with an integrated flux or special types for use with other metals. It may be just a matter of personal preference, but a separate solder and flux generally work better. Flux can be bought in two forms, a thin liquid or a grease. There's little to choose between them so, again, it comes down to personal preference.

Which metals can be soldered?

Most metals can be soldered after a fashion, but brass has become the norm because it is versatile and responds so well to soldering. It is also the most available in a wide variety of forms (sheet, rod, tube and so on) and is relatively cheap. It is not as easy to bend as copper or aluminium, but this can work to advantage in keeping lengths straight. As we will see, its brittleness also helps when cutting it. Copper wire may lend itself to 'organic' constructions such as branches, but the results can be a little flimsy. Because copper is such a good conductor, copper rod requires a lot of continuous heat to solder it effectively. Both aluminium and steel can also be soldered, but this is rarely done because it is problematic, requiring special solders and fluxes.

Soldering equipment, consisting of a soldering iron with stand, solder wire, flux, sponge, metal files, steel wool, and wet & dry paper. Also showing a work in progress.

METAL VERSUS PLASTIC

It is worth asking: Why use metal at all? The brass bedstead shown here as an example could conceivably be made from thin styrene rod, 'welded' using either styrene solvent or superglue (methods using styrene and other plastics are covered in Chapter 2, 'Constructing'). At the least, the bed ends could be styrene, although the connecting frame would be too weak to support any pressure. Cutting and assembling styrene would certainly be far less involved than using brass. The styrene could be given a pretty convincing brass look in a variety of ways. Perhaps even a combination of soldered frame and styrene details could be considered, because styrene can be glued reasonably well to brass (provided that the surface of the brass is 'keyed' a little, that is rubbed with wet & dry paper to clean and slightly roughen it). Before styrene became so available in model shops soldered metal was the only option for something so thin in scale, but styrene is now commonly used whenever possible. However, one of the most useful, perhaps irreplaceable qualities of metal, is that it can be smoothly bent into a shape which it will then hold fairly rigidly. This makes it a suitable choice in the case of the bedstead for some of the curved elements of the design and is certainly the only practical choice for bendable armature constructions.

Example 1: a brass bed

1. As with any design/making task, this should begin with a scale drawing to establish proportions, detailing the design of the headboard and footboard and including a side view to show the frame length. This is by no means unnecessary effort, because, especially with soldering, the design really has to be worked out as fully as possible beforehand. It is not possible simply to add bits on or alter the proportions once assembled. This should be adopted as a general rule whichever material or method one is using. As I have said, most of the skill of model-making takes place in the head (as opposed to the hands) in the form of visualization, planning, anticipation and problem-solving. If the object is to be reproduced full scale at a later date (as in the theatre), a detailed scale drawing will be needed in any case. It is much easier and more accurate to design things of this size in 1:10 scale, reducing them on the photocopier as required.

2. Keep the drawing safe by pasting photocopies onto a piece of foamboard with Spray Mount (Pritt or similar can be used if spread evenly). The foamboard serves as a flat, stable surface which will not warp with the heat of the iron and will also protect the work table. It will also act as an insulator (very similar to a polystyrene cup), meaning that it will not draw heat away from the work being soldered. The mounted drawing will be the 'jig' upon which the components of the bed are constructed.

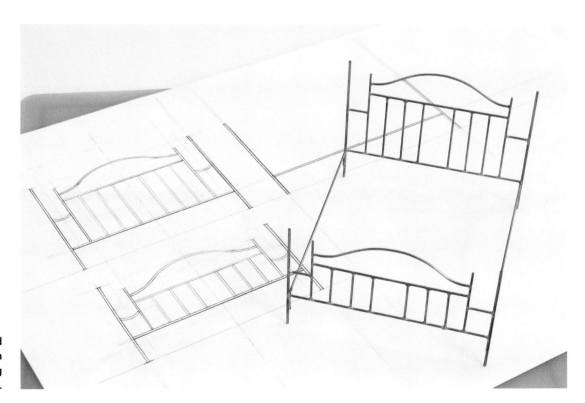

The brass bed assembled, with the drawing underneath.

3. Prepare strips of brass first (in this case, 0.8mm thickness has been used to represent the structure at 1:25 scale) by rubbing with steel wool or wet & dry paper. This is essential because any dirt, grease or protective coating must be removed in order for the flux and solder to work. It is far easier to do this before cutting the brass into its individual pieces, but care must be taken not to bend the straight rod in the process.

4. The brass can then be cut into the required lengths to construct the components. For brass up to about 2mm thick this can be done with a scalpel. Keep a few old blades in order to do this. The brass rod used here was first nicked with the scalpel at the points where it needed to be cut, placed on the cutting mat and then rolled under the scalpel blade, pressing down fairly firmly. By this means, a small groove was made right round. Care must be taken to keep the blade at a right angle to the brass while doing this, otherwise one ends up with a spiral line. The groove made doesn't have to be very deep, but certainly defined. You will be able to snap the brass at this point by grasping it firmly with pliers close behind the cut and bending the rest. This method gives a much straighter cut than side cutters and it is easier to judge exactly where to position the cut.

MAKING A CUTTING JIG

A number of straight elements for the bed ends shown had to be cut exactly the same length to fit properly between parallel bars. In this case, it saved time to make the simple 'L' shaped cardboard jig shown. This acts as a set guide for the scalpel cut, saving measuring and marking out each time.

This method also works for square-section rod, although here it can't simply be rolled under the blade. But just one firm groove scored into one side should normally be sufficient to make the metal break at that point. It takes a little practice to find out how much of a groove needs to be made for rods of different gauges. Here, the slightly brittle nature of brass works to our advantage and it also means that the brass is likely to stay straight along its length even though the end of it is being forced. Copper, being much softer, tends to bend out of shape before snapping. Sheet brass up to a certain thickness can also be cut by scoring and snapping in this way.

Using a simple cutting jig.

The bed-end pieces taped to the template ready for soldering. Photo: David Neat

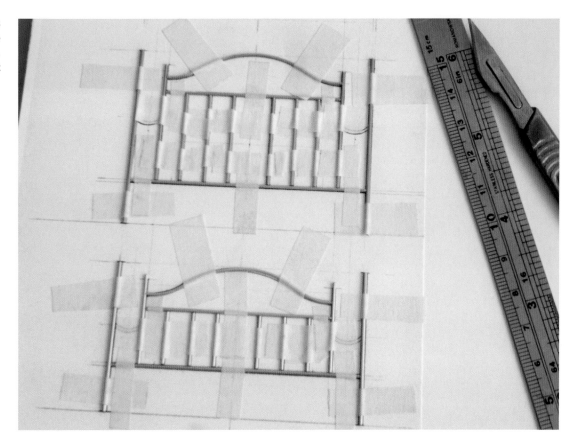

5. Once cut to size, the pieces can be firmly taped into place on the drawn template. It is important that they all fit flush with each other, that is, making maximum contact with no gaps. Jagged ends should be filed as flat as possible using a metal file and where shaped ends are needed these will also need to be filed to fit. Thin strips of masking tape are best for securing. These should not be placed too close to the points being soldered. Double-sided tape could be used, but unfortunately the glue will soften very quickly under the heat of the iron so unless you're very quick your carefully positioned pieces will shift around too much.

6. Apply a little flux to a joint, making sure that the joint is being covered and little else. A small brush is best for this. You will need two hands for what follows, which is why the work always has to be provisionally assembled and secured before starting. Incidentally, the soldering iron needs a few minutes after being plugged in to reach a working temperature. Once it is ready, place the tip of the soldering iron on the metal as near as possible to the joint but not directly over it. It is essential to 'straddle' the joint, touching both pieces at once. Holding the iron firmly there, take some solder wire in the other hand and touch the end of it to the joint. What should happen is that a little of the solder melts, flowing into the joint. If the metal is hot enough, the softer solder will liquefy and be pulled into the joint

gap by capillary action. The tighter the fit, the less solder will be needed to fill the gap and the stronger the joint will be. Blobbing extra solder around the joint won't make it more so. On the whole, this is true of any kind of bonding using any kind of adhesive.

If none of this is happening, there could be a number of reasons. Either the soldering iron is not powerful enough to heat the thickness of wire used, or it needs a rest for a moment to regain temperature, or dirt on the bit is impeding the flow. If the solder is melting but forming droplets rather than running into the joint, then the joint needs to be cleaned with something abrasive or more flux needs to be applied. As a last resort, try placing the soldering iron tip almost over the joint, touching the solder directly to it and letting the solder melt from the iron onto the joint. This may assist, but will only work properly if the metal itself is also hot enough. Often a technique known as 'tinning the iron' is helpful, which consists of putting some flux on the iron tip once hot, melting just enough solder onto it to form a thin coating and then using the iron as normal. The layer of solder helps with the transfer of heat.

7. Once cool enough to touch, the work can be detached from the template and any excess solder easily filed off with a metal file if necessary. One last thing is essential before this stage of the job is complete. The flux is a

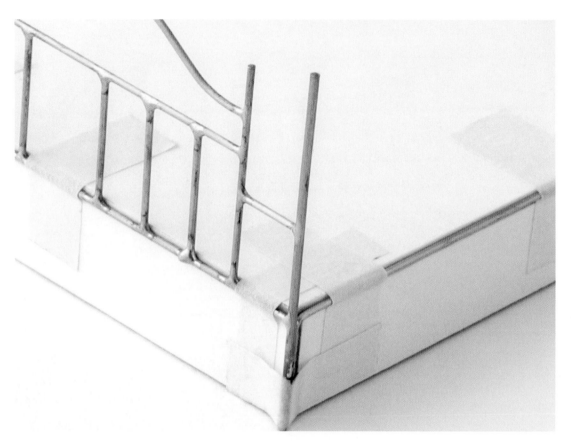

Detail showing the box, or jig, needed to hold the bed ends firmly upright while joining them with a frame. The joint here is a stronger lap joint.

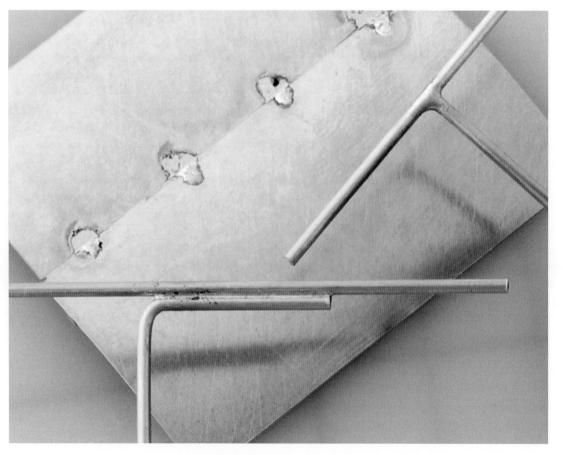

Different types of joint. Below is a stronger overlapping or lap joint with the finer but weaker butt joint above. A common technique for joining sheets is to spot-solder at intervals.

corrosive substance which, if left on the metal, would slowly eat into the surface and weaken the joint. If any permanency is needed, the work would need to be scrubbed carefully with water and detergent (or warm vinegar) to neutralize the flux. An old toothbrush is useful for this.

8. So far, we have soldered on the flat, but to make the complete structure head and foot need to be connected to a frame. These pieces must be held firmly in the right place before being joined and this can be done by taping as before, although the template now has to be three-dimensional. In this case, a box has to be made which will give support both to the completed bed ends and to the pieces of frame joining them. Everything needs to be taped down securely, especially those parts nearest to where the frame will be attached, because as these are heated up again neighbouring joints may loosen.

Whereas the two ends of the bed were made by simply soldering cut pieces end-to-face, the frame should ideally be a little more strongly attached. Here it helps to form a lap joint by bending each end to be joined to include a small right angle, which means there will be much more surface contact and the solder can run the length between the surfaces rather than remain as a spot. Joints like these are much stronger than the butt joints making up the bed ends and should always be made where possible, for example where they may be hidden, as here. It is more difficult to get exactly the right length with two bent-over, rather than cut, ends, so enough extra brass should be allowed for a little trial and error.

Example 2: figure armature

The figure armatures shown consist entirely of these lap, or overlapping, joints. These joints have to be strong because the armature is made as a flat piece, similar to the bed

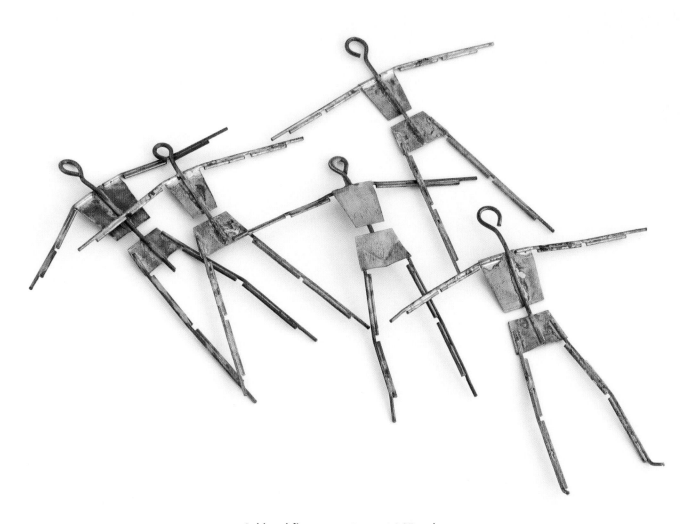

Soldered figure armatures at 1:25 scale.

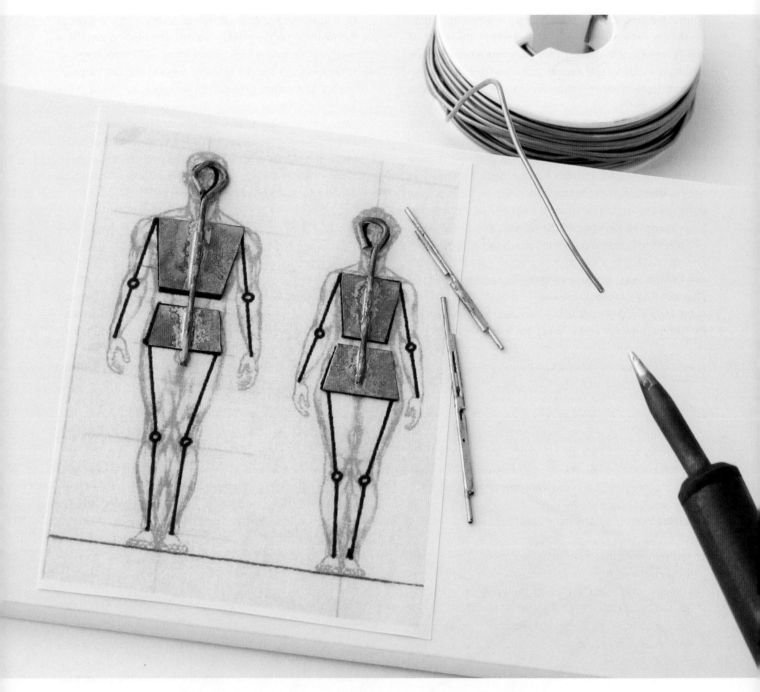

Figure armatures being soldered using drawn templates.

components, but then bent into position. The principle is taken from stop-motion puppetry, where if a simple wire structure serves as the skeleton this is at least reinforced on the portions of the limbs where you *don't* want them to bend, leaving the joints free. When the puppet's position is changed during animation, the limbs will automatically want to bend where the joints are supposed to be.

The adaptation here is not recommended for stop-motion

puppets, however. Brass will only take a certain amount of bending and here it serves for establishing a pose which, allowing for a little bit of repositioning, will remain fixed once the modelling material is applied. The idea was developed for static 1:25 figures.

1. The first task was to draw up a clear figure reference (for example, with the help of an anatomy manual for artists)

and to reduce these to the required scale. The draft setting on the printer was useful for producing a faint image on which the armature shape could be designed. In doing this, it was important to keep in mind how the real human armature, the skeleton, is positioned within the body. It was helpful to find skeleton references and reduce these to the same scale. For example, the bones of the shoulders are close to the surface so the armature is taken to the edge of the drawing. Similarly, with the bones of the leg, they run closer to the outside than the inside and the joints to the pelvis are quite far apart.

2. Having drawn up the framework, it can be copied and pasted onto foamboard and the pieces then cut according to steps 1–4 of the previous example. Shapes for the torso and pelvis were cut out of 0.1mm brass shim (available from sculpture suppliers, used for building 'fences' round a clay prototype for mould making). The torso and pelvis are connected along the centre by the same strip of brass which loops to form the head. Each limb is a straight length accompanied by shorter lengths which will be attached to keep those parts of the limbs rigid. A few millimetres are allowed for joining to pelvis or torso and to form the basis for hands and feet. For this scale, 0.8mm brass rod proved to be strong but still bendable.

3. When soldering the parts together it is easier to attach torso, pelvis and spine together first, make the four limbs separately, then solder them to the trunk spread-eagle fashion. Once ready and cleaned, the armature can be bent into a position.

What can then be done with these armatures is properly described in Chapter 5, 'Modelling'. Here they serve as an example, together with the soldered bed and the other cases that follow, of the usefulness of being able to work with metal. One tends to think of metal only when trying to solve a functional, constructional problem, particularly when something thin, strong or bendable is required, but metal can also serve a more decorative purpose illustrated by the following.

Metal etching

For centuries, printmakers have been developing different ways of using chemicals to dissolve the surface of a metal plate so that these areas will take ink which can then be transferred to a sheet of paper when the two are pressed together. This process is known as etching. The object of the process is to control exactly where the chemical bites into the metal and this could be done in its simplest form, for example by coating the metal plate first with something that resists the corrosive action of the chemical. If this layer is then scratched away in parts, only those parts would be etched and nothing else. So a drawing of considerable detail could be scratched into the coated surface, those lines would be etched, printing ink rubbed into them and the whole drawing transferred as ink to paper.

Many other ways have been developed over the centuries of transferring a drawn design onto a metal plate for printing – the most widely used today involves a photographic process. The metal plate is coated with a photosensitive emulsion by means of which an image can be transferred to it, which can then be processed to resist the action of the etchant.

Printed circuit boards (PCBs) are produced by etching a pattern in thin copper, but in this case all the way through. If metal sheet can be dissolved all the way through, instead of just on the surface, then the possibilities are at once opened up for making structures out of thin metal just by initially drawing them. More than that, if the metal need not stay flat once etched but can be bent into three dimensions, the possibilities are further extended. It is simple to draw directly onto a metal sheet with an etch-resist marker pen (these can be bought from any supplier of materials for etching circuit boards, such as Maplin in the UK, but any waterproof permanent marker should work just as well). However, there is a limit to the level of detail that can be achieved by hand and the final result is a one-off. To make the technique pay, it is better to have some means of reproducing the image. I have chosen to explain a medium-difficulty technique here that I have found most effective for some tasks. It is much more versatile than the one-off, but not as complicated as the photographic method.

Materials and equipment needed

Once more, brass comes out on top as the best choice of metal because of its availability and price, but also because a thin sheet will retain its flatness while still being bendable if necessary. But it's more a question here of which metals prove easiest to etch using available chemicals. Brass is very easy to etch, but so is copper. Model shops are the best source of sheet metal, if rather expensive for the sizes offered. A cheaper source of sheet brass is sculptors' shim (the same used for the figure armatures earlier), which is usually 0.1mm thick.

The choice of metal will determine the choice of etching solution, or etchant. None of the suggested chemicals are dangerous in the red-letter sense, but care must be taken! They are corrosives, although salts rather than acids, and while they affect metals they have less effect on the skin. However, as a safeguard rubber gloves should be worn when working with these chemicals. What one does have to be cautious of are the

For the tropical rainforest model shown here in detail, David Lazenby reproduced a variety of specific leaf forms using the brass-etch method. Photo: courtesy of Lazenby Design Associates

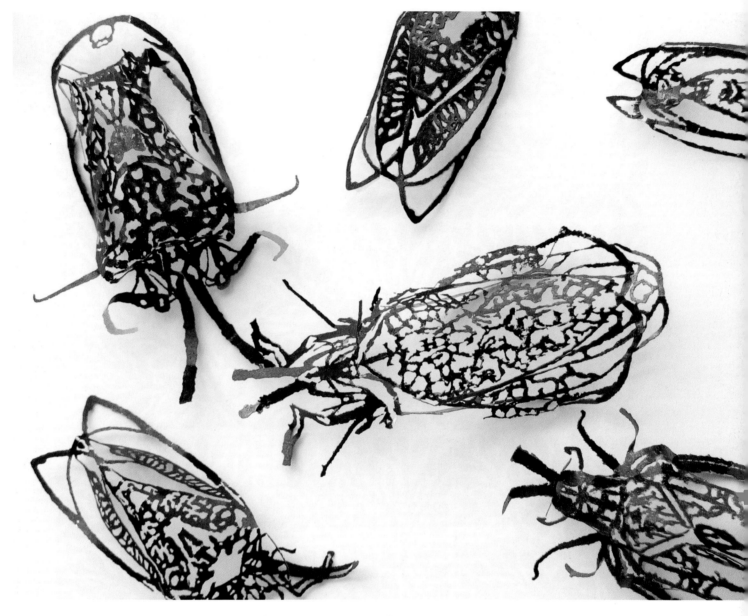

Beetles by Astrid Bärndal. These designs were transferred to thin brass sheet by means of Lazertran Silk paper and then etched through using sodium persulphate.

fumes and so good ventilation is essential. They will also stain (and eventually eat holes in) some fabrics. They must be properly disposed of when no longer needed and not just tipped down the sink! Suppliers of materials for home PCB making will usually stock two chemicals suitable for etching through thin copper – ferric chloride and sodium persulphate. Both work just as well on brass, because it is an alloy composed of copper and zinc.

The simplest, most effective method of transferring drawn artwork onto a metal surface in the form of a resist is to photocopy the image onto a transfer paper such as Lazertran Silk. The image is made by whatever means, hard black on white, but then colour copied onto the transfer paper. The reason why it's important to make a colour copy rather than black and white is that the black produced in colour copying is high in toner. The latest forms of black and white copiers use a different kind of ink, which is not effective and neither unfortunately is inkjet ink. It is the toner (a fine meltable plastic dust) which will transfer and stick to the metal surface and resist the etchant.

I have listed only the particular materials required here. Other standard ones necessary for the work will be apparent from the step-by-step account which follows. There may be many

The A6 artwork composed of repeated leaf units.

applications for this home technique, but 'organic' patterns are the most suitable. The reason is that this simplified method involves etching from only one side, whereas factory etching is done from both. The process therefore takes longer and the edges produced will be slightly more ragged. Factory etching makes use of much higher concentrations of etchant and a heated solution, which takes a matter of minutes, whereas this will take hours. If reliable results are needed to a deadline, it is better to have one's artwork etched commercially, although this can be pricey!

Example 3: foliage

Trees and plants are notoriously difficult to achieve with any realism. Usually even the best renditions in scenic models stop at suggestion rather than accurate facsimile. On the whole this is the best approach and if materials are chosen with the right sense of scale and given the right colour treatment the results can feel remarkably real. But the following method is worth considering where time will allow, or where a very specific detailing of foliage is necessary.

1. The artwork has to be created first, black on white, whether by hand or using a digital programme. Since Lazertran Silk paper comes in A4 size and the price can work out at over £1 a sheet, it makes sense to cram as much as possible into an A4 format. On the other hand, etching a metal sheet of this size can be impractical (plus sculptors' shim comes in a smaller size). For this reason, I usually divide the layout of the A4 artwork into four A6 areas with a little gap in-between, not forgetting that there also needs to be a few millimetres of space around the outside for the printing margin. For this example I chose to draw a squared unit of leaves by hand, which could then be scanned, opened in Photoshop and repeated to make an A6 block. This is in turn repeated four times to fill an A4 page. It is, of course, easier to draw at a larger size and reduce later to the scale required.

2. Once the artwork is ready it can be colour-photocopied onto a sheet of Lazertran Silk. The first hurdle perhaps is finding a sympathetic copy shop which is prepared to use special papers in their machines. Not all of them will, but those used to catering for the unusual requests of artists and designers will be more amenable. The copy is made on the shinier side of the Lazertran paper and it's worth asking at the shop for the best possible contrast.

3. Once copied, the A6 block can be cut from the page, keeping fairly close to the edge of the design. The sheet metal should be cut to a size just a little larger, perhaps up to

1cm all round. The surface of the metal will have to be thoroughly cleaned on one side first to remove any grease or protective coatings. It's best to use steel wool, water and detergent for this.

4. The following part of the process can vary in success. Heat is needed to transfer and melt the photocopy toner onto the surface of the metal. This can be done either by heating the metal sheet in the oven and quickly rubbing over the Lazertran paper (copy side down) on the surface, or it can be done by ironing paper and metal with a hot iron. The manufacturers of Lazertran Silk recommend a temperature of 180°C. If using an oven it's best to set the gauge a little over 180°C and leave for ten minutes. The metal should be put on a baking tray, which should be removed with it and remain under it in order to ensure that the metal remains hot while the paper is applied and rubbed. Oven gloves are essential, as is a tissue or cloth with which to rub the paper. If an iron is used, the procedure is simpler but extra care must be taken not to move the paper while ironing. Whichever source of heat is used, a bowl of hot water needs to be standing by in which to immerse the paper once the image is stuck. If all goes well, the paper part will detach itself of its own accord leaving the toner print on the metal, although it may need to be carefully peeled off once it is soaked. The plate must not be left in the water for long because water may start to get underneath the toner. After the plate has been left to dry out naturally it must be put back in the oven for another few minutes to ensure that the toner image is properly melted on the metal.

5. Now the metal plate with the resist image on it can be prepared to be etched. Commercial metal etching usually involves aligning the image and etching from both sides, but that is not possible with this simpler method. The back of the metal will therefore need to be masked and low-tack Frisket film is best for this purpose. The metal should be edged with Sellotape front and back to complete the seal. If any details of the design have become damaged they could be corrected using a waterproof marker.

6. Sodium persulphate was used to etch these examples. It can usually be obtained as a powder from any specialized electronics shop selling PCB etching supplies. The dry crystals need to be dissolved first in the right amount of water to make up a solution. Directions may vary, but in this case 200g of sodium persulphate was added to 1ltr of warm water and agitated occasionally until all the crystals had dissolved. A plastic tray is needed for the etching bath and polypropylene food containers are often an ideal size for an A6 sheet. The prepared sheet should be fully submerged in the solution. Patience is needed now because the etching process can take a good few hours. Small bubbles will start

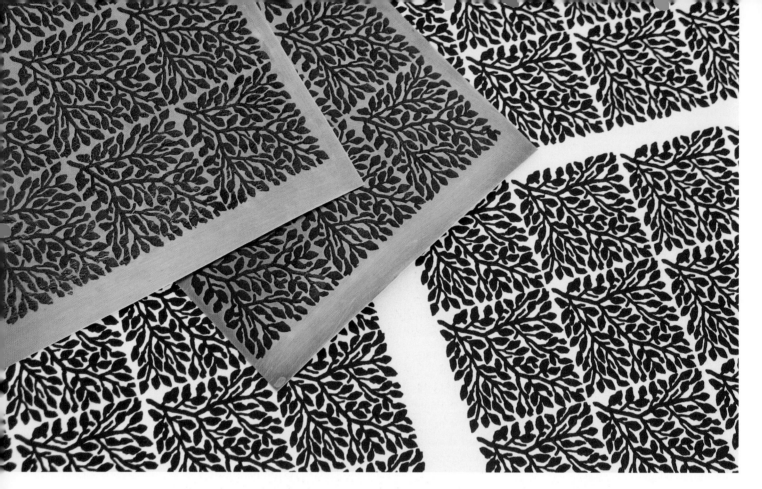

ABOVE: **Prepared A4 sheets of Lazertran Silk with A6 portions transferred onto brass.**

BELOW: **Small bubbles appear on the metal surface once etching has started.**

Usually after a couple of hours parts of the metal have been etched through.

The individual leaf clusters, some already bent into shape.

to gather on the metal surface and after a while the solution will turn increasingly blue.

7. Progress should then be checked at regular intervals to make sure that the sheet remains immersed. It also helps to agitate the solution each time. Etching rarely takes place uniformly with this method, which means that some parts may be etched too much (the etchant starts biting into the edge of the pattern), while others need longer. This is

another reason why organic patterns work best with this method, because the difference is less obvious. When finally ready, the etched sheet must be thoroughly rinsed and the components can be carefully detached from the low-tack plastic film. These should be rinsed again for good measure. Etchant can be reused many times over until the solution is totally spent, but the process will take longer each time.

ABOVE: Attaching the leaf patterns to the tree form. The best method of doing this is to use superglue and accelerator.

RIGHT: The tree completed and painted. A combination of enamel greens has been used to paint the foliage.

Metal Mesh

After rod and sheet, another useful form that metal comes in is mesh. The variations are again seemingly endless, ranging from fine woven, or punched and expandable, to welded grid forms. Dedicated model shops should stock a variety of the finer forms, while the larger ones can usually be found in the garden sections of DIY centres (such as B&Q or Homebase in the UK). Fine woven meshes (usually steel, copper or brass) could be used to simulate stretched gauze curtains in theatre models and their rigidity is sometimes a help, but on the whole a fabric version such as organza is more manageable, much easier to colour and a lot cheaper.

The punched, expandable meshes are much more interesting and versatile. They are made by punching repeated slits into thin metal sheet. This sheet can then be stretched and the slits become lozenge-shaped holes. Soft metals such as copper or aluminium are perfect for this. The resultant sheet can almost be modelled by pushing and pulling and it will take simple impressions of objects because the individual 'cells' can expand or contract in almost any direction. This is often sold as 'impression mesh'. Because all the strands are connected, it can be cut into any shape quite cleanly with no fraying.

This type of mesh offers a perfect solution for draperies when something a bit sturdier than metal foil is needed. The mesh is first cut to size, that is, the full extent of the curtain is stretched flat and tissue paper can be spray-mounted or glued onto both sides. This can then be shaped to suggest the folds of a curtain. It may be easier to lay the mesh onto something soft such as a folded cloth and press the stock of a paintbrush into it to form folds. Small landscapes can be fashioned by similar means, except that the shape must then be properly supported underneath because it will remain fairly fragile on its own. Different gauges (sizes of mesh) are available appropriate to the delicacy or strength of the form needed.

Welded wire mesh is composed of a gridwork of wires (usually galvanized iron), which are welded together at each intersection. It is a larger-scale, coarser and tougher material than punched mesh, without any of the latter's mouldable properties. The type known as 'chicken wire' is not welded, and is more suitable for larger-scale landscape modelling. Whereas welded mesh may be limited in its uses as a sheet material here, it is invaluable as a source for pre-welded wire structures. The following example will demonstrate the best application, but other forms are possible, for example chairs or even simplified figure armatures.

The outline form for the tree is first cut from the sheet and snipped in the appropriate places before the shape is pulled out and bent using pliers.

Example 4: a wire mesh tree

A size of mesh has been chosen that is suitable for fairly small trees at 1:25 scale. It is made up of wire welded in 12mm squares. It is pretty universal and available from most DIY or garden centres. The basic principle is that the wire can be snipped at the appropriate places to create a simple tree form as a flat cut-out, which can then be bent into a convincing 3-D shape using pliers.

1. It is best to start by planning where you are going to cut. Since the material is cheap and the method is relatively quick you should make some trials first, to give yourself an idea of how cutting the wire in certain places will lead to certain shapes when pulled into 3-D. It won't take long to appreciate both the possibilities and the restrictions. It is better to draw out an initial plan on a 12 × 12mm paper grid, lay the mesh over it, and mark the cutting points on the metal with a thin red marker. Otherwise it's all too easy to get lost!

2. The wire can then be cut with cutting pliers (an individual tool rather than the cutters on combination pliers). The metal is soft enough to do this without much effort. You may prefer to wear something like gardening gloves because the cut ends can scratch.

3. Once the shape is cut, you can start to bend. Only a little can be done with the fingers; mostly you will need pliers and it is best to have both a standard-size flat-nose pair and smaller round-nose ones (*see* the 'Tools' section of the Directory of Materials). The results are more effective the more straight lines one can eliminate, even for the end-most branches, and the more multidirectional one can make the overall shape, the better. The photo shows a rather generic tree, but other shapes are possible.

The completed shape.

Further stages in tree creation. Above, reticulated foam has been glued to the frame and crushed eggshell completes the effect on the right.

The painted tree. The trunk has been left untreated. Sculpey is the most convenient material for thickening this up.

Detail of painting.

4. An effective means of representing foliage (for scales larger than 1:100) is to use reticulated foam and crushed eggshell. The individual cells of this foam have almost disappeared, leaving a latticework of filaments. Clumps of this can be glued to the metal using PVA (the rough surface of the wire will allow this). You may choose to paint the metal before doing this. Crushed eggshell is a good medium for representing leaves because the particles are flat rather than rounded.

5. The painting stage needs a special mention here, in addition to Chapter 7, 'Painting'. The green of the leaves should be varied, otherwise the result will look dead. Here the different colours of the eggshell were utilized, using in this case green inks to tint them instead of paint.

CLADDING WITH SHEET METAL

Standard aluminium foil could be used to cover small areas requiring a metallic finish, although this is difficult to keep smooth. The colour can be modified, that is, made darker or given a gold look by painting with FEV (French enamel varnish), or a clear varnish to which a little colour has been added. Smoother cladding is possible using the thicker foil found on food containers. Hobby shops sell thin copper or brass foil by the roll, sometimes with an adhesive backing.

Model caravan made by Marie Antikainen as part of a set model for *Peter Grimes*, a project at Rose Bruford College, Kent. Stiff aluminium foil from food containers has been applied to the side and baking foil covers the top. Photo: David Neat

CHAPTER 5

MODELLING

As stated at the beginning of Chapter 2, 'Constructing', models are far more assembled than sculpted, which is why this chapter is separate and also why it is relatively short. It deals with some of the exceptions, for example instances of forms for which the assemblage of cut sheet or carved block just doesn't work, usually because in real life these forms have grown rather than been built. Forms such as trees or human figures need a different approach – that of 'pushing a soft material around'.

Since modelling in this context is more a case of copying a predetermined shape, especially in the case of the human figure, rather than embarking on the kind of 'free-fall' sculptural trip experienced with an abstract form, it becomes more of an exercise in 'guided restraint', or 'planned limitation'. The more ways one can find of making the armature do most of the work, or using templates to guide the modelling, the better. There is room for the fluid, spontaneous and accidental of course … but this tends to be somewhat unreliable!

Tools for modelling

The best modelling tools are our own fingers and it is surprising how much detail can be achieved with them even at a small scale. We are so used to using them on their own to manipulate things and our fingertips are especially acute in their sense of pressure. As soon as we have something in our hand, such as a tool, we lose a lot of that control and sensitivity and craftspeople might spend a lifetime trying to bring it back. However, for modelling figures in 1:25 scale, for example, something is needed to impress more detail than the fingers can. The simplest and cheapest option would be to modify some cocktail sticks and coffee stirrers using a scalpel and fine sandpaper. It is useful, for example, to have a blunt or rounded end in addition to a sharp one, also both a flat and a round-ended spatula shape. Needle files (intended for fine metalwork) also make good modelling tools, but only when using a non-sticky material such as polymer clay, otherwise they will be rendered useless for anything else.

Serious modellers may want to invest in some professional modelling tools or spend a bit more time customizing their own. In the former case, it is better to have some standard clay modelling tools (for initial work and larger effects), together with a few dental modelling tools. Particularly useful is the type of clay modelling tool composed of a fixed wire loop, invaluable for removing rather than just displacing clay.

Modelling materials

The two modelling materials featured in this chapter are Super Sculpey (a polymer clay) and Milliput (an epoxy putty). They are, between them, fully representative and there may be no need for anything else. Space is confined in this chapter to describing techniques rather than materials, so more about the materials (together with some alternatives) can be found in the 'Modelling' section of the Directory of Materials.

Example 1: modelling figures

The challenge of figure modelling generally tends to separate the sculptors from the designers, although I am not suggesting that the two are mutually exclusive. But those who enjoy using material to create form will usually like it, whereas those for whom the model is merely the necessary means to a larger end will probably not.

If one is trying to do the job properly, and irrespective of the materials that are going to be used to create the figure, one has to start by at least mapping out the essentials of the figure in a drawing. This should include both a frontal and a side view and these should be drawn in the same scale and aligned with each other. It is much easier (as with model furniture) to make these drawings in a larger scale first and then reduce them to the final size. Both sets of drawings can be referred to while working; the larger showing more detail and the smaller defining the size.

ABOVE: Architectural constructions can be assisted by a variety of mechanical means but the more organic components can only be modelled by hand. Charlotte Hern modelled these façade elements using the modelling materials Milliput and Sculpey. Photo: Rachel Waterfield

LEFT: These tools have been hand-made out of a strip of walnut. The wood is hard and durable, but easy to carve and sand (tools made by Astrid Bärndal).

The most versatile material for the purpose (and for almost any small-scale modelling purpose) is a polymer clay called Super Sculpey, because of the ease with which it can be worked. Sculpey is already a film-industry standard for figure maquettes because of its consistency and relative price. It has the softness and elasticity of plasticine when kneaded between the fingers, but without the annoying tendency of plasticine to stick to the fingers when warmed too much. All polymer clays have a very similar composition and can even be mixed with each other. The manufacturers of polymer clays (Sculpey, FIMO, Cernit and so on) recommend that their products are baked in a domestic oven in order to harden them. This is a simple process involving relatively low temperatures, but almost any source of sustained heat will have an effect (the examples in this chapter were all hardened using a heat gun). Oven-baking can get tricky if the oven is inconsistent. Tests should always be done first to establish the correct setting. (Take small pieces of clay and roll one paper-thin, the next a bit thicker and so on, up to around 25mm thick. Bake these in the oven together for about fifteen minutes at the recommended temperature of 130°C. Examine the results when cooled.)

Another virtue of Super Sculpey is that the same piece can be baked over again without further effect (provided that the temperature and baking time remain reasonable). This means that a form can be modelled in stages and each stage can be hardened before applying the next. This solves the problem that

often occurs when modelling something soft, that of pushing the form out of shape while trying to model details on top. It also solves the equally frustrating problem of where to hold a small form while completing another part of it. This may not be an issue in conventional sculpture where the size of the figure dictates a rigid armature on a fixed base, but it is difficult to work on a small-scale figure in this way. It needs to be hand-held to get to every part.

1. Before modelling can begin a wire skeleton or armature has to be made, even for figures at 1:25 scale. One method for producing a versatile and accurate form of armature in soldered brass is detailed in the previous chapter. These basic armature constructions (one for a typical male, another for a female) can be bent into any position to suit. A good armature is not just a support to stop the clay sagging – it should also be a proportional reference, a sculpting guide, an indication of how far to go and where to stop. Getting the armature right constitutes perhaps more than 50 per cent of the effectiveness of the figure.

2. Instead of working directly on the armature with Sculpey and modelling the figure in one go, a thin mannequin is first made using Milliput. This is an epoxy putty mixed in two equal parts which allows about forty minutes of working time under normal conditions. Milliput is much stickier than Sculpey, so it can be used to coat the metal armature

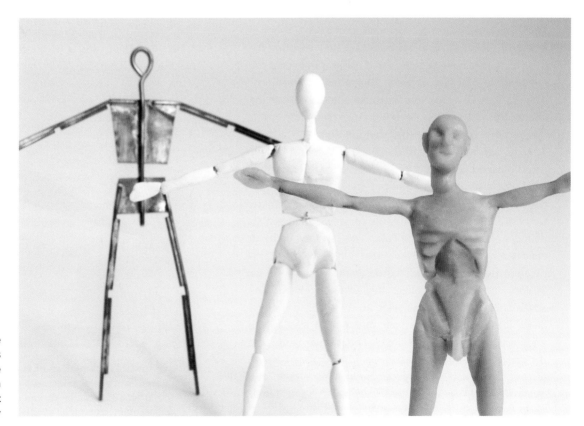

Stages in figure modelling. The brass armature, the halfway mannequin stage and the first layer of Sculpey

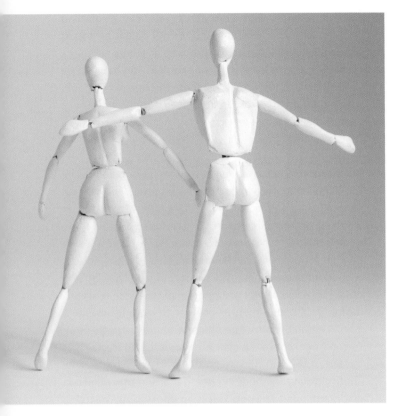

The fine, white version of Milliput was used for these mannequin figures. Joints are still left free at this stage for repositioning later.

firmly (*see* the Directory of Materials for a fuller account of Milliput). Once set, it will provide a better base for the detailed modelling in Sculpey and it will also withstand the temperature of 130°C required to harden polymer clay. Unless you have a clear and fixed idea for the pose of the figure, it is best to keep the positions of joints free at this stage so that the pose can be arranged later.

3. Sculpey can be applied to the Milliput before it is fully cured if need be, but it is best to wait a few hours. If you are in more of a rush the Milliput could be skipped altogether and Sculpey used for the thin halfway stage. Getting the Sculpey to stay on the metal will require a little more effort, but it can be done. This can then be hardened quickly using an oven or a heat gun (if the oven temperature does not exceed the recommended 130°C for Sculpey it should not affect the soldered joints). The advantages of this halfway stage are twofold. In the first place, it encourages some basic attention at least to the underlying anatomy of the figure. The wire armature was the skeleton; now simple muscles are being added. In the second place, soft Sculpey can be pushed around too much if left on its own. Each layer needs some firmer backing.

4. The advantage of being able to harden portions or layers of Sculpey successively is that one can complete the modelling on one half of the figure, fix it and then work on the rest without fear of damage. The same can be done purely in Milliput without the need for heat, but this would involve longer periods of waiting. This kind of modelling is better achieved without too many breaks in concentration. One can gradually develop both a feeling for the material and a feeling for the shape and proportion while working, but the mood established can just as easily be broken. It is often better to make all the figures one requires at the same time.

The basis of effective figure modelling lies (as with everything else and even for figures at this scale) in observation of the real thing and the collection of clear references. When modelling figures we are both aided by, but also battling against, familiarity. We are so used to seeing human heads, for example, that we don't properly *look* at them. One has to start by being fairly specific about what one wants, rather than hoping that the figure will somehow emerge in the process. Like many things, modelling a figure is 'all in the preparation' and there is nothing harder than trying to achieve a convincing result from a vague, imagined notion. A good understanding of anatomy is invaluable for a start, though perhaps not at that level of detail prescribed for larger-scale work. There are many good books devoted to figure modelling and some are listed in the Bibliography here. How one models – how one manipulates the clay into particular shapes – is very much a personal thing and can only be discovered through practice.

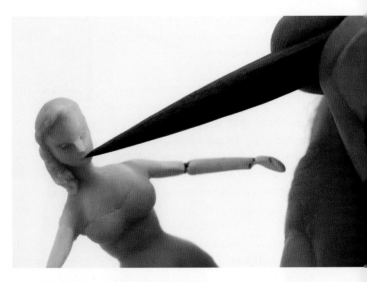

Working towards completion of modelling on one area. Some details are easier to achieve once the Sculpey has been hardened. It can be carved or shaved with the scalpel, as well as sanded or drilled.

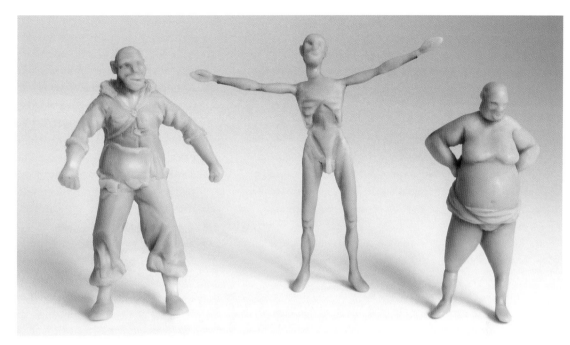

A group of almost completed figures. At this small 1:25 scale, it may be better (and it's certainly easier!) to move towards caricature or simplification rather than attempting to be too realistic or elaborate.

RIGHT: Detail of one of the figures painted. At this scale, more is achieved by broader effects.

Example 2: modelling a tree

If one can achieve some confidence in modelling reasonably good figures, everything else is simple by comparison. One method of creating tree shapes was introduced in the previous chapter and that method could be used for the armature in place of the method here.

1. The armature in this case has been made by taking a number of equal lengths of florist's wire, twisting them tightly together to form the trunk and dividing them up to form the branches. Proper florist's wire is relatively soft and pliable because it has been annealed. The uncoated variety is recommended here and this is often sold in packs of a certain length. If this proves difficult to find, aluminium wire is the best option. This is even softer, but the Sculpey will provide enough rigidity when hard. In this model, fourteen strands have been twisted together. The advantage of this method, that of starting with a bunch and then dividing them, is that some of the work involved in starting with a thickness of trunk and thinning out branches occurs naturally. Note that some extra length is needed at the base if the tree is to be slotted into a baseboard.

WORKING WITH SUPER SCULPEY

The following tips on using Super Sculpey are worth noting:

- It should be stored away from sources of heat, such as radiators or the sun, because even mild heat may cause it to start curing and harden.
- The surface can be cleaned and partially smoothed with methylated spirits, although this should not be allowed to dissolve it (similar to smoothing earth clay with water). Meths is useful if you need to degrease baked Sculpey before painting.
- If you find the material too soft to work with, make a flat pancake and press between two sheets of absorbent paper (normal copy paper will do). If this is left overnight the paper will extract some of the plasticizer and the clay should become a little tougher. Alternatively, you can use talcum powder when handling to reduce stickiness, but on the whole stickiness, unlike plasticine, is not a problem.
- If old Sculpey has become too tough, there is a clay softener obtainable from the manufacturer which can be mixed into it.
- The best work surfaces to use are melamine, Formica or ceramic tile. Sculpey will continually take the grain from wood, the wood will absorb some of the plasticizer from the compound and wood dust or splinters will gradually build up in the Sculpey.
- If an oven is used for hardening the Sculpey, it should go in the middle on a baking tray covered with baking paper, or ordinary paper. Avoid foil as this will leave its impression on the clay.

- When its time is up in the oven (or when you have finished with the heat gun), the clay may not appear to have changed in colour and it will still feel rubbery to the touch. This doesn't mean that it isn't 'done'! It will complete its hardening as it cools down and the colour will usually (but not always) darken.
- Be aware that if the clay is overheated or burnt, the fumes are toxic! Care must therefore be taken not to overheat it.
- The same pieces can be re-baked many times without damage (as long as the temperature remains the same). This means that complicated forms can be modelled in stages. Fresh Sculpey will adhere well enough to baked Sculpey and if not a little PVA glue can be used to help. This doesn't affect the baking.
- Baked Sculpey is painted best with acrylic. Enamel paints should only be used if the form is primed first with Simoniz primer, as any oil- or polyurethane-based paint or varnish will react with the polymer. If a varnish is needed it should be acrylic or alcohol-based.
- Sculpey glues excellently with superglue, forming a strong bond. If repositioning is needed, or if gluing parts which don't fit tightly, you can use an epoxy glue such as Araldite. Weldbond or even normal PVA might also work.
- Once baked, Sculpey can be carved, sawn, drilled and so on without fracturing. It sands very well, although it is difficult to sand to a totally 'industrial' smoothness without using a filler. Polycell's Fine Surface Polyfilla is best for this.

2. Sculpey can then be modelled onto the armature, with the twists of the wire helping it to stay in place. This can be done in one go, or built up in layers as described in the previous example.

3. For the same reason that building in layers is recommended for the figure modelling, it is easier to harden the Sculpey at this stage and model a texture separately over it. The photo shows a section of trunk that has been partially clad with a bark formation. The thin layer of Sculpey is much easier to manipulate or impress without fear of distorting the general shape.

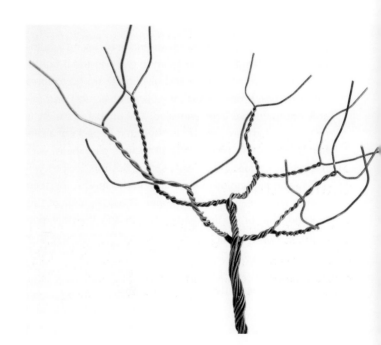

The wire armature.

The armature covered with Sculpey.

Modelling the texture of the trunk.

Example 3: rock formations in Sculpey – 'impressing rather than pushing'

This little piece was used to illustrate a simple method of casting in Chapter 3, 'Methods of Casting'. As such, it needed to remain fairly simple in form, with minimal overhanging, and an emphasis on clearly defined surface textures rather than shape. Having looked at some real examples of rock surfaces and having a basic idea of the shapes they generally break down into, some objects were collected that could provide interesting ready-made textures. Here one has to first imagine the negative, but this can be quickly tested on a piece of clay. Textures especially will often come out very differently in reverse from what one imagines.

1. Because it is important to keep the distortion of the general shape to a minimum but still be able to press quite firmly, a rigid core shape of polyurethane foam is first put

The rough core of Kapa-line foam. Superglue has been used to assemble it.

The finished form with impression tools.

together, roughly 2–5mm smaller all round than the intended piece. In general, unless one wants to remain flexible with the basic shape, the more complete the core form or armature, the better, even on objects this small. This practice is essential in product model-making, for example where an almost full-size car model might be fashioned in clay. Often a skeleton framework is welded in steel, on top of which polystyrene or styrofoam is carefully shaped to within a few centimetres of the car's actual size. This is referred to as the 'blank'. Lastly, styling clay is applied as an even coat over it, ready to be shaped smooth. This is not only to save on the amount of styling clay needed, but also the foam is a rigid support which controls and eases the shaping of the clay. In the case of these rocks, the blank could have been simply fashioned in Sculpey and then heated, but the foam is much cheaper by volume. Polyurethane foam will withstand a certain measure of heat (the Sculpey layer will partly protect it), but this is not guaranteed with other foams.

2. Sculpey is then modelled over this blank. It helps to smear Sculpey thinly into the foam in places first so that it will stick better. Once the whole has been covered, more Sculpey can be added to eliminate the sharp angles, gradually building up a more natural form.

3. The photo here shows the modelled form together with the tools used to impress shapes or textures into the Sculpey. Lines and fissures are made by running or just pressing the edge of the dental modelling tool shown.

A vignette featuring 'Greed' from the automaton 'Esther & The Great Davamaska' by Elves 'n' Elements, a model-making/prop/creature effects company based in Elstree. The modelling is in Sculpey and the repeated forms were press-formed using moulds.

Textures can be filled in by hand in this way, although the results can look too deliberate and artificial. It is much better to utilize other things and generate some 'controlled accident'. Here, the choices include a piece of reticulated foam, some wire mesh, a piece of bathroom loofah and some aluminium foil. Each will create different impressions that can be used in combination. Aluminium foil is particularly versatile for impressing (when fashioned into a block or point), because the scale and shape can easily be altered.

4. If foam is used for the core, it is better to place the finished form on a ceramic tile and use a heat gun to harden it. If this has a setting control it should be set to medium, held about 10cm from the work and run for about one minute, turning the work constantly. If by the end of that minute the Sculpey is just too hot to keep your fingers on it will be enough. Whereas the recommended oven heating will bake the Sculpey right through, this method may leave some clay at the centre unbaked. Under normal circumstances this will not be a problem.

Modelling in relief paint

This technique is featured here because it is more a case of 'liquid modelling' than anything else. Relief paint, sometimes marketed as 'dimensional paint', can be found in some hobby shops for applying embossed decoration to cards and ornaments. The firm DecoArt produces it in a range of colours. Raised lines or patterns can be drawn on card or plastic and these will shrink only minimally as the substance dries. It will

The prototype for the cast frieze featured earlier was made by piping polyfilla onto a photocopied template.

accept acrylic paint or enamel. This technique is not only useful for suggesting relief mouldings on walls or picture frames, but also for giving flat model furniture more dimension or decoration.

An alternative is to make one's own relief paint – Fine Surface Polyfilla from Polycell is most suitable for this. The polyfilla only needs to be mixed with a little water to make a smooth paste (the consistency of yoghurt) and then introduced into any squeezable plastic bottle that has a thin nozzle through which the mixture can be piped. It is important to mix thoroughly because any lumps will impede the flow when the mixture is applied (this may take a little while because this type of polyfilla will behave like cottage cheese when water is first added). An alternative might be to use a good quality acrylic texture paste similarly 'cut' with a little water.

Suitable bottles to contain and apply the mixture can be found in most toy shops. The one shown in the photo originally contained a water-based glitter paint that was easy enough to clean out. Some art or hobby shops sell empty plastic bottles for a similar purpose.

The larger-scale frame section on the left was made by piping successive layers of polyfilla onto the plastic template. Each layer is allowed to dry before the next is applied. A surprising depth can be built up in this way without the need for cutting and carving.

CHAPTER 6

CREATING SURFACES

Personal preferences

Are you someone who likes to build up or to break down? Do you prefer to utilize a found surface such as a textured paper or to work from scratch? Do you tend to want to keep surfaces simple and make the paint effects do most of the work, or do you prefer it when the texture facilitates the painting? You may say quite rightly that it all depends on what kind of surface is required and that you might employ a different technique for each individual case. However, that option depends on your knowing the full range of what's possible with a wide variety of materials. Generally, people tend to stick to favourites and those they have had most experience with. Their choice may be a reflection of something within the individual personality and integral to other aspects of that person's work.

We've already examined one specialized method of creating surface effects – making latex skin casts in Chapter 3 – and touched upon another – using Kapa-line foam – in Chapter 2. These are my personal preferences. I tend to try to make Kapa-line foam do whatever I want, regardless of whether there might be an easier method, just because it's familiar to me. However, it's never too late to become acquainted with something unfamiliar and hopefully this chapter will encourage that.

It also depends a great deal, of course, on what you have to hand, because whereas materials for construction are usually anticipated beforehand and bought in specially, materials for surfacing tend to get overlooked until the time comes. In order not to just 'make do' with whatever happens to be in the studio or in the kitchen, a well-stocked arsenal of possibilities might read as follows:

- *Fillers:* polyfilla, acrylic texture medium.
- *Special papers:* textured vinyl wallpaper, sandpaper, velour, marbled papers, embossed prints.
- *Scatter materials:* granulated cork (fine, medium, coarse), vermiculite, sand, poppy seeds, mixed herbs.
- *Cladding materials:* obeche wood, cork sheet, Kapa-line foamboard.

The question of how accurately a surface should be represented in scale is an important one. Take sand, for example. If we were to represent it exactly to scale, grain for grain, we would have to use a powder so fine that it would have no visible texture at all. The way sand as a mass is shaped by wind or water is another matter, but the basic texture of flat sand is best represented by fine sand itself or fine sandpaper, regardless of the fact that this is not strictly true to scale. A road or pavement surface of asphalt is a similar case. We can see that it has a certain texture, but at the scale of 1:25 this could, strictly speaking, be accurately represented using paint alone. Yet the effect produced using something with more depth, such as a painted sandpaper or lightly stippled polyfilla, is somehow more satisfying and looks more realistic.

If one nevertheless feels the need to be more specific with scale, it's sometimes difficult to judge how prominent a texture should be. Even with something as small as a 1:25 chair the thicknesses of individual parts are measurable and, patience willing, controllable in the model. It is more difficult to measure and control the average depth of a texture in the same way. An easy answer is to say that one acquires a 'feeling' for the right scale in model work over time. While this is true, it relies on regular model-making and so doesn't help much at the beginning. One possible solution is to take clear, flat-on reference photos of common surfaces, preferably at times of the day when the light accentuates them. These should be taken with a tape measure or metre rule in view. They can then be printed out at a good resolution, but with the size adjusted to conform to whatever scale one habitually uses, referring to the measurement gauge either to reduce or enlarge the image. Having them around while creating a texture is at least a step in the right direction.

Using fillers and pastes

The brand name Polyfilla has become a blanket term in people's minds for a range of products, which, although they promise to do much the same thing, will differ considerably in their

A combination of subtraction and addition was used to create the effects of corrosion on this 1:100 model of a wrecked ship made by David Lazenby. The styrene build was broken down in places using a Dremel tool and fine sand was added to paint for further texturing. Photo: courtesy of Lazenby Design Associates

Good, clear reference photos are an essential basis and it is far better to source a surface and take photos yourself. Here a measuring tape has been included to leave no doubt about size. Photo: David Neat

A page from a surfaces sample book showing different effects in Kapa-line foam.
The labels contain details of how the effects were achieved.

MAKING SAMPLES AND KEEPING THEM

An important thing to remember when using a found texture or creating one from scratch is that changing the colour can dramatically alter the appearance of the texture. It is impossible to visualize, for example, how cork mat will look when painted a uniform white, or how a stippled polyfilla surface will change when it's darkened. It's even more difficult to anticipate the effect of washes that will give a tonal variation, or the dry-brushing effects dealt with in the next chapter, 'Painting'. In this context it is therefore essential to make test samples before committing to a solution. In the case of creating a surface stippled in polyfilla, for example, it is important to make more than one test of the same effect, just to ensure that you are in full control of the process, which can vary a lot, simply with the angle of the brush.

Having taken the trouble to make these samples one might as well keep them for future reference, although they are useless if not archived in some handy form including notes on how they were done. There needs to be a conscious commitment to this because it is often the last thing one wants to think about when struggling against a deadline. But the effort in producing a well-documented sample book will be justified not only in terms of one's own future reference, but also as inspiration and as an aid in dialogue with other people. These samples should not be too small and should be kept to a similar size. It's easier to appreciate them if they're mounted on a fairly neutral colour or black. Whenever possible, it's best to include a little of the painted and the unpainted texture for comparison. The notes may have to be detailed if the surface was created in a specific way, for example in the case of stippling a texture medium, what kind of brush was used, whether the medium was diluted, how many coats, whether the surface was sanded afterwards and whether anything else such as sand was added to the mixture. This may not be obvious from just looking at the sample later and it's best not to assume that you will remember all the details of how it was done.

Illustrating the variety of effects achievable with just a filler. These have been spread, stippled, impressed with a textured sponge, scraped or sanded. Painting with a thin wash will bring out the texture.

Samples of foam surfaces partially painted, with the 'tools' used to texture them.

behaviour. Anyone who's achieved a specific effect in one type and then tried the same using another will know this. Some fillers (speaking just of the ready-mixed ones) have a higher water content than others and so will only properly adhere to porous or properly 'keyed' (roughened) surfaces. They may shrink or crack more when drying and will be reduced almost to a dust at the mere suggestion of sanding. Others may be gritty, hence difficult to smooth out or stipple with, and they will harden like granite.

The texture samples opposite were achieved with one of the most versatile of the bunch, Fine Surface Polyfilla, which is made by the original manufacturer, Polycell. It is much more like an acrylic paste than a plaster. It will stick to anything, even plastic, although it may be wise to key the surface a little by sanding. This adhesive property will remain even when thinned with water and it can also be used as a gap-filling glue, particularly between porous materials (*see* Chapter 5, 'Modelling', for a short account of using this type of filler as a relief paint). It can be spread very smoothly and when dry can be sanded to an eggshell finish if need be. Like most water-based fillers, there will be some shrinkage (though far less with this type), so if a covering of more than 1mm is needed it is better to do this in stages. Each layer will have to dry thoroughly before applying the next. It dries relatively quickly, although there is still ample time to work with it while wet.

However, the main benefit of using this kind of medium is not as a body filler, but for direct texturing. Different textures can be created according to what one uses to apply the filler, for example a palette knife, toothed spreader, brush, sponge roller or fingers. Other effects can be created by using something to imprint the surface while it's still wet, for example stipple brush, damp sponge, metal mesh or specially patterned rollers. This only works properly if the filler will 'stay put' in the pattern that's left and not sink or shrink into flatness. It also helps if the sponge or patterned roller is dampened, preventing too much polyfilla from sticking to it. Patterns can be created on a sponge roller surface either by pulling off pieces of the foam or melting away lines with a heated wire. Care should be taken to avoid any fumes produced if this is done. The various impasto media or texturing pastes available to use with acrylic paints work very well and are worth considering, but Fine Surface Pollyfilla will perform just as well at a fraction of the cost. This type of polyfilla is also very stable once it has dried and can be easily sanded, scratched or carved with hardly any crumbling.

Some fillers are supplied in powder form to be mixed when needed. This can be an advantage because they will keep for a long time, whereas the ready-mixed versions tend to dry out however careful one is to reseal the plastic container. Putting a little water on top, sealing the lid with tape and wrapping the container in polythene may help with this. Although the powder form works out cheaper, using the ready-mixed is more practical and ensures that the mixture will be the same consistency for repeated work.

Defined areas of the foam surface can be pushed down to create slightly different levels or a layered effect, here using the end of a metal ruler.

Alternatives to water-based fillers

Epoxies, for example the car body filler available from car accessory shops, may have some advantages but an equal number of drawbacks. They do not harden by evaporation but by chemical reaction and come in two parts (either two pastes or a paste with a liquid catalyst), which have to be mixed thoroughly in the right proportion in order to harden. This they do very quickly, which can be a drawback if you need the time to texture them, but is advantageous on a tight deadline. They will generally dry hard and tough, but can be sanded to a super-smooth finish. The fact that they do not rely on evaporation means that they will not shrink, can be applied in much thicker layers and can make a very good gap-filling glue between some materials. They are much more expensive and some wastage is inevitable when mixing in small amounts. Good ventilation is needed as they will give off a lot of vapour.

Using Kapa-line foam

Whether the special qualities of the foam layer in Kapa-line foamboard are used as a form-making basis, as described in Chapter 2, 'Constructing', or whether they are just used to make a surface, the range of things that can be achieved is impressive. Styrofoam, which is also available in very thin sheets, will perform in a similar way, but it is not as impressionable and comes with a very slight surface skin that really needs to be sanded off before it will do all the things illustrated here.

There are two drawbacks which need to be considered before using foam sheet to create surfaces. The first is that it usually has to be planned from the beginning of construction rather than added as an afterthought because the thickness of the foam will alter the dimensions of the piece. The second is that the foam surface will always remain quite sensitive and may be a risk for pieces which need to be handled or transported a lot. Paint will toughen it a little and this can be increased by priming with PVA or an undercoat, although these will also alter the texture. If untreated foam is painted with a thin matt paint, the effect can be very deep, rich and totally non-reflective. It may, of course, be that you want something smoother or glossier, in which case the foam would need to be filled with a coat of polyfilla. If the polyurethane foam is left completely unpainted it will change over time from a fresh, subtle ivory to an old yellow ochre due to the effects of light and the surface will begin to powder slightly. Although the foam itself is light and soft, the polyurethane powder produced by sanding is hard and relatively heavy so it will not hang in the air. However, care should be taken and a face mask worn if sanding large amounts. The powder can also be abrasive, so sensitive skins could be irritated and special care should be taken not to rub it into the eyes.

When stripped of its covering paper, the surface of Kapa-line foam can be interesting in itself. Sometimes it's a little rough where the paper has taken some of the surface with it and this could be used as it is to suggest flat concrete or broken asphalt. This can be enhanced by lightly stippling some polyfilla, just enough to sit on the surface without filling it. If this 'sits up' too much, it can be sanded flatter using a fine sandpaper. None of this is an exact formula and results will vary, so you have to be the judge of whether it is appropriate. If the surface needs to be broken down further, wire brushes can be most effective, either by stippling or by 'scumbling' (rocking the brush around while pressing) to produce a deeper, pitted surface. The small wire brushes intended for cleaning suede shoes or the tougher ones for removing rust are useful for this process.

Sometimes a simple combination of techniques is needed to create an effect. In the example opposite, the irregular surface of layered rock is suggested by first lacerating the surface in all directions with a sharp tool. Small portions of this pattern are then pushed in using the end of a ruler. These indents will stay where they are and will not expand again with painting. This is, incidentally, a good way of suggesting old, broken paving stones without having to piece individual squares together.

One of the most effective uses of Kapa-line foam is in solving the problem of model brickwork. There are other methods that can be tried, for example stippling polyfilla through a finely cut (or etched metal) stencil, scoring soft card or thinly layered polyfilla, or making a latex skin cast. However, the foam method is likely to prove quicker, easier, more effective and more versatile. The photo illustrates this method.

First of all, the area of wall needs to be marked up with the horizontal mortar lines. It makes sense to draw up a template for a particular scale, mount it on something durable and keep it for the future to mark from rather than having to start over with the scale ruler each time. A mechanical pencil is the best tool for inscribing lines on the foam. Pressure can be varied to produce a subtle indentation or a deep crack, depending upon the type and age of brickwork to be represented. Strictly speaking, if you look at brick walls you will notice that the mortar lines are rarely set deeper than the bricks themselves; in fact, they're often a little bit proud of the surface. However, creating the general effect by scoring will give a better definition in the model and more importantly the pronounced pattern will be an aid to painting.

Having scored all the horizontal lines, vertical divisions between the bricks are required to complete the effect, but these are less easy to put in quickly because they need to be staggered. The simple home-made tool shown, consisting of a run of teeth cut in 0.5mm styrene mounted on a more rigid

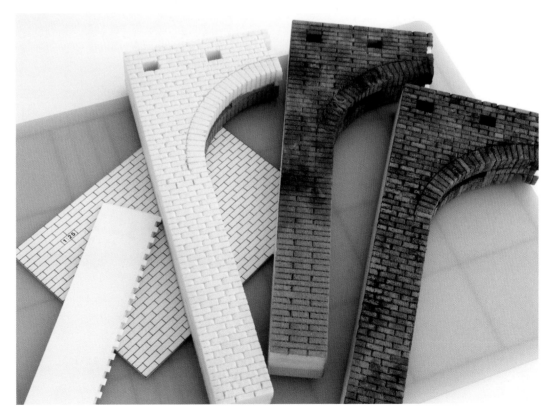

This brickwork arch piece was first constructed in foam, then scored all over with a brickwork pattern. It makes sense to draw up a permanent measurement template for brickwork, especially if always working to the same scale. The toothed tool lying next to it is a time-saver, custom-made out of styrene and used to impress vertical mortar lines. Stages in painting are shown, including a basecoat and dry-brushing the pattern.

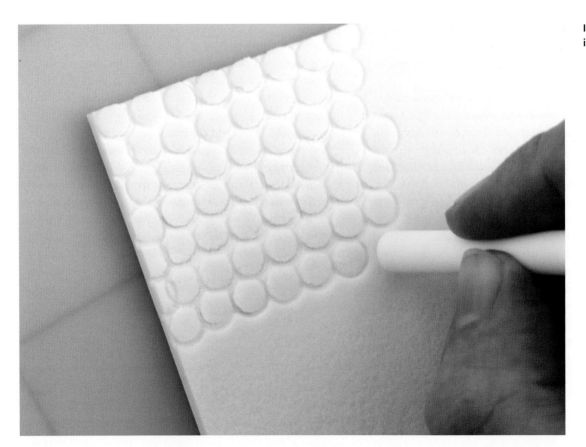

Impressing a pattern into Kapa-line foam.

Here squares in the foam have been sliced right through using a sharp scalpel blade while keeping the knife at a right angle. They can then be inset and secured at the back with PVA.

support, will make the job much easier. These teeth are spaced so that they will make a vertical groove in every alternate line when the comb is pressed into the foam, making it possible to put in whole rows at once.

The added advantage of using sheet foam is that the continuation of the brickwork around corners can be made seamless – can be a problem if using something harder. If a modern brick wall is being conveyed, only very light scoring may be necessary. In ancient or decayed walls the bricks might recede in places, so certain areas should be pushed in with a flat tool. The whole surface can also be attacked with a wire brush to give a more crumbly appearance.

The photo on page 111 showing samples of partially painted foam surfaces includes an example of simulating cobblestones. For this, a tube of the correct size was found (an old spray diffuser proved to be perfect, or aluminium or brass tube can be bought) and pressed repeatedly into the foam surface. It is the reverse, or positive version, of the method used on the foam to create the latex skin moulds in Chapter 3, 'Methods of Casting'. It helped that the ends of the diffuser tubes were all slightly

different sizes, reflecting the variation that cobblestones often have. Other 'tools' can be found to create an infinite variety of effects in this way. The surface of the foam can reproduce a surprising amount of detail, as you could test for yourself by pressing a coin into it.

Another method of creating a more prominent and sharper relief pattern (though more a method of construction than texturing) is to slice shapes, such as squares in this example, cleanly through with a scalpel and instead of removing, inset them slightly. They can be secured at the back where they protrude by brushing the joins with PVA.

Using special papers

Making use of found papers to represent surfaces can be particularly labour-saving and will open up possibilities that are difficult to achieve by any other means. However, care must be taken because it is easy to fall in love with a particular effect,

A selection of decorative papers including 'marbled' writing paper and embossed patterns.

forgetting the scale that it will become in the model. The range of possibilities and the places to look are so numerous that only a few examples can be suggested here. Art material shops are a good source for many and it is worth looking at the heavier watercolour and oil painting papers. Oil painting paper, for example, has a fine, fake canvas imprint which could be useful for giving life to flat painted areas. More on this is included in Chapter 7, 'Painting'. But for the fullest inspiration it's best to see what a more specialized outlet such as Paperchase has to offer, or to browse through the sample books of Falkiner's in London. Here you will find an excellent range including printed, marbled, fibred, hand-made, translucent and embossed papers. Many of these originate from the specialist firm E. Becker in Bedfordshire. Stationery shops are also worth checking for the variety of writing papers now available. The 'parchment' or marbled type, which can usually be found in a variety of colours, may form a perfect base for reproducing a marble surface in the model.

The local DIY centre may not be an obvious source of interesting papers, but it will be the best for two in particular, sandpaper and vinyl wallpaper. I've already mentioned that fine sandpaper could be the best option for representing a flat, sandy surface. It will most probably need to be painted, in which case it's far better to use a matt enamel or airbrushing acrylic, because normal acrylic will fill the texture. Coarse sandpaper could form a good basis for pebbledash or gravel, although used on its own the effect would be too flat and regular. It should be brushed with thinned PVA and sprinkled with extra, loose sand to build up the effect. Textured vinyl wallpaper can be particularly impressive! There are many varieties of 'organic' pattern and a centre such as B&Q will have an opened roll of each available to take samples from. Even parts of the woven or floral patterns may have their uses. This paper is meant to be painted and even thinned acrylic will cover it well, but it is also interesting to note what a very thin wash will do. The raised vinyl pattern will resist watery paint but the paper underneath will take it, resulting in a definite tonal difference accentuating the pattern. If this pattern appears too sharp or regular, it can always be softened by coating with a layer of thinned polyfilla.

For the model overleaf, based on an old abbey and used as a theatre prop, textured vinyl wallpaper was cut into strips, glued to a plywood build and given a wash of thinned enamel. Because the model was never seen close-up, only a suggestion of stonework was needed and the vinyl texture proved very resistant to handling.

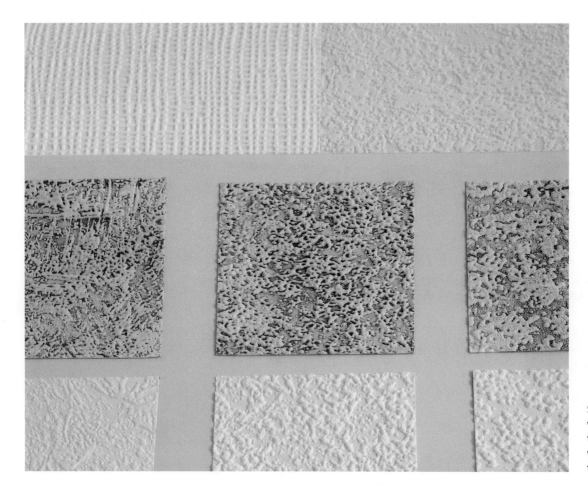

Samples of vinyl wallpaper showing the effect of a thin wash to emphasize the textures.

Strips of vinyl wallpaper used to suggest stonework on a prop model. Since it was only meant to be seen from a distance, textured acrylic glass provides a good enough impression of the glazing. Photo: David Neat

Cladding materials

Wood

As in the case of representing sand, one would expect that the most effective material to use to suggest the quality of wood is wood itself, provided that a thin enough version can be found. It is, after all, the right base colour and can be stained to make it darker. The grain is already there and staining will accentuate it. Thin sheets of it can be easily cut and layered to represent wood panelling or profiled mouldings. Like plastic but unlike card, edges can be softened or rounded by sanding. Of course, for working at small scale the finer the grain and pattern of the wood the better, because the sense of scale can be disturbed if these are too prominent. The most common sheet woods available from model shops (such as obeche, walnut and bass) have a fine enough appearance to work at almost any scale. Obeche

ACHIEVING REALISM WITH THE GRAIN

A common mistake when attempting wood panelling or panelled doors in the model is to forget that the real thing is composed of many parts fitted together and the grain of the wood will almost always follow the longest side of any rectangle. So, in the panelling shown, for example, the grain of the bottom panels and any other continuous horizontal strips will run horizontally, while the grain of the upper panels and the spaces in-between will run vertically. This is one of the things that gives wood panelling its distinctive look and, though laborious, the model should be similarly constructed.

An ensemble of stained wooden surfaces mostly using obeche wood, with unstained tables for comparison.

is the most versatile, being softer and less brittle than walnut but more available than bass. The grain is also more interesting without being too prominent and straight cuts are possible without the blade becoming 'diverted' by the grain.

Cutting any of these into intricate, especially curved, shapes might prove a problem, though, firstly because the grain will tend to divert the scalpel blade along it and secondly because the wood can easily split. Covering the back with masking tape while cutting will help a little. Alternatively, good model shops will stock a selection of extra-thin, smooth-surface plywood sometimes referred to as 'modeller's plywood'. Because the outer veneer is bonded to one or more inner layers where the grain follows a different direction, this is unlikely to split so easily, making it ideal for intricate cutting. This plywood can be as little as 0.5mm thick, but it can also be expensive.

Wooden floorboards deserve special consideration, if only

because the results vary alarmingly! Not wishing to encroach upon aspects of design, care must be taken at least to check how wide floorboards normally are and what type of wood is used. It should also be checked how prominent the spaces are between them and how breaks along the length are usually arranged. All these will vary according to the period and the style of building. It may not be enough just to judge what looks right in the model. Breaks in the planks are necessary because planks are not usually as long as rooms, but these breaks can only occur in reality where the ends can be secured to a sub-structure, so they can't be just anywhere. One might ask 'Who's going to notice?', but if an impression of reality is the aim, it is surprising how only a few minute departures can undermine a convincing effect.

Obeche is generally the best wood to use for cutting floor-board strips because it is fairly smooth-grained and easy to cut straight. Modern pine floorboards usually have a more prominent grain (or resinous streaks), which can be quite nicely simulated in model form using thin spruce. Another recommendation that may seem even more annoying is that planks for the model should be individually cut, rather than gluing a whole sheet of wood down and scoring lines in it afterwards. The difference is very perceptible! If a collection of strips is cut and the planks jumbled before being stuck down, especially changing the direction lengthwise, the planks will look more varied, as in real life. This will be much more apparent when the wood is stained because the differing surface naps will take the light in different ways. But when considering using stained wood it is important to make some colour tests first before too much time is spent inlaying a particular wood. It may be surprising how any unseen structure in the wood is brought out by staining. This photograph of the sample section also shows how a lighter wood may not necessarily stain lighter; here, the bass wood has accepted more of the stain and has become much darker.

If the cracks between are accentuated it is better to mount strips of wood on black card, otherwise unsightly white lines will remain when the wood is stained and these will be impossible to fill. A common headache, particularly with respect to floors, is warping. This can occur either when gluing the strips into place, or when the whole floor is washed with a stain. In the first instance, if PVA is used it need not be spread uniformly on the underside of the strips. Small dots of glue will suffice to hold these in place and this should prevent too much warping. A quicker and even cleaner alternative would be to lay diagonal strips of double-sided tape at intervals over the area to be clad and fix the strips this way. In the second instance, using a spirit-based rather than a water-based stain will guarantee that there's no warping. The only danger here (apart from the vapours) is that if this is used liberally and soaks through to the double-sided tape it will start dissolving the glue. A foolproof solution might be to glue with dots of PVA but to colour with a spirit-based stain.

A sample section of floorboarding partially stained. The strips have been jumbled and both bass and spruce have been included on the right to vary the appearance further. Care needs to be taken to avoid glue spots which will interfere with the stain.

Creating the effect of wood, using coarsely sanded PVC for the floor and stencil paper for the furniture.

Delicate panelling using brass rod glued to a mountboard surface.

Alternatives to wood

Real wood can be very satisfying to use but sometimes rather time-intensive. In Chapter 3, 'Methods of Casting', a 'wooden' chair cast in resin is featured; this can be made to look just like wood if properly painted. All it needed was the suggestion of a grain which was then emphasized in the painting. A similar quality can be given to PVC or styrene by scraping with coarse sandpaper. Being softer, PVC can be given a very prominent 'grain' in this way. This needs to be coloured with a thin paint, so that the grain effect is not lost. More on the painting technique is included in the next chapter, 'Painting'. The illustration opposite features a section of faked wooden floor in PVC, unpainted at the top. The advantage of using plastic in this case is mainly speed. The lines between the individual floorboards were scored on the surface (so no need for a separate base-

board) and the whole area was scraped, altering the pressure and direction in places to give some variety. This technique might be particularly useful for curved or intricate elements, which would prove very difficult using real wood.

Also included in this photo are the panelling element and simple furniture made from stencil paper featured in Chapter 2, 'Constructing'. Here they have been stained with a standard wood stain to look more like wood. Just because something is made of wood doesn't necessarily mean that the grain will be prominent or that it will be noticeable at a small scale. What counts more in this case is a subtle variation in the overall colour helped by the faint mottling which the stencil paper already has. A careful coat of satin varnish can complete the suggestion.

It's often difficult to convey the delicacy of wood panelling, especially if thin, rounded strip mouldings are involved. Here,

A collection of earth effects using coloured polyfilla as a base. The surfaces have been painted in places to suggest drying mud. The top sample is composed of used teabag tea, bound with PVA and with some fine grit and eggshell thrown in.

Ground samples featuring grass, using dyed sisal pressed into polyfilla. Other plants have been added using coloured sawdust.

the effect is achieved using brass rod that has been carefully glued to cardboard. If the brass is cleaned with steel wool, thinned PVA will hold it in place and should be brushed over the surface for extra measure before painting. This example has only been sprayed with a grey primer, but painting first in a basic wood colour and then adding a darker wash or stain can create the desired wood effect.

Simulating earth and grass

Although it might seem like stating the obvious, there are many different types of earth and just as many different formations of grass. Earth can differ greatly in its appearance, depending upon whether it's freshly dug or solidly compact, whether it's softened with moisture, or hard and dry. Different localities also have their special signature, whether of colour or texture. The same goes for what we generalize as 'grass'. There may be many plants included in the general effect which are not strictly grasses and what appears at first sight a unified carpet is in fact a mixture of forms and hues. If earth or grass has to feature in a model, these specifics have to be addressed and researched. This may seem like a lot of bother, but it will make the job easier in the end. There's nothing harder than trying to create a generic, all-purpose and imagined surface

and expecting to end up with a truly satisfying or convincing end result.

It is rare to find an earth which is a completely unified, single substance. For this reason one should rarely use just straight filler, such as polyfilla, to represent it. It's always better to mix something else into it, such as sand, fine grit or granulated cork, which will make the mixture clump in much the same way that earth does. Alternatively, the powdered tea from used teabags makes for a different and interesting consistency. Whatever one uses, a general recommendation is to colour the mixture to at least the right base colour before applying it. This will save painting it later and will prevent white areas showing up if the surface is damaged at any time. Acrylics can be used, although this can be a bit costly if you are making a large amount of 'earth' because it will take a lot of paint to turn white filler into dark brown. The concentrated toners available for colouring emulsion paint are probably a better option for this; these can be found in most good paint shops. What improves the realism of the samples shown is a sprinkling of 'stuff' – a little coarse sand, some mixed herbs, finely crushed eggshell, some railway modeller's gravel and the like. Most earth has small stones or dead plant material in it, even bits of pottery and brick. It is also worth breathing a little more life into the subject by means of painting. Here, a little white was mixed with the original colour and dry-brushed to suggest places where the earth was drying out.

The grass featured here was created using a special, but simple, technique, using the sisal mats that garden centres sell to line hanging flower baskets. The sisal fibres are compacted rather than woven, so they can be pulled out in clumps and, what's more, they are often dyed grass-green. For these samples, an earth mixture was made up and coloured as previously described. This was spread quite thickly onto the base and small clumps of the sisal were pressed one-by-one into it. Only small areas can be done at one time, otherwise the polyfilla will start drying out. The more compactly the sisal is arranged, the fuller the grass effect. Once the polyfilla is fully dry (this should be left for at least a day), much of the sisal will still be loose and has to be teased out, but what remains will still provide a thick cover and can be trimmed down with scissors.

Soft furnishings

Carpets, curtains and upholstery are included in this chapter because getting them right is often more a matter of surface than form. Once again, Kapa-line foam proves itself invaluable here. If cut to shape and sanded with fine sandpaper it makes a perfect surface for upholstery or cushions. If a thin matt paint is used, the foam surface looks very like a soft fabric. If needed, the foam can be pressed using something like a cocktail stick to suggest creases. Curtains could be created in a similar way,

carving or sanding folds with a round file. Although this method may be a little painstaking, it allows for more control over form and scale than the usual method of soaking a very thin fabric in glue or paint, arranging its folds and hanging it to dry. It would be difficult to achieve the detail shown using this method. But another method which allows as much control and is quite popular is spray-mounting tissue paper onto aluminium foil. The foil can be crumpled or creased into a fixed shape and the tissue painted. This is perfect for something like sheets on a bed, for example, because the foil can be pressed to drape convincingly over the form underneath.

At a little risk to your printer and only if it can take the thickness, there is a way of printing an image onto tissue paper in order to make curtains with a properly scaled pattern. The pattern image is first created in Photoshop or a similar digital program in the manner described in the next chapter, 'Painting'. Tissue paper is carefully spray-mounted (using the repositionable kind) onto a sheet of acetate, smoothed as flat as possible and the edges trimmed. This can then be fed through the printer and the printed tissue paper peeled off and glued to the foil.

Another fairly common problem is how to convey carpets convincingly. A colour photocopy of an actual carpet will be inappropriately shiny and will probably also feel too intense. An inkjet print on ordinary paper may work better. Further to this, if the image is first reduced in pixel count and then enlarged, the resulting pixilation may enhance the suggestion. It helps if

Detail of a 1:25 set model by Ben Stones for *Paradise Lost* (Oxford Stage Company). The drapes have been intricately carved in foam and then painted. Photo: David Neat

Both armchair and sofa have been made almost entirely out of foam, then treated differently. The armchair was left slightly rough and given a thin wash, while the sofa was more thickly painted and polished for an old leather look. Here, the carpet is a piece of oil painting paper rubbed with some colour.

This pebbledash surface could be represented using coarse sandpaper but the irregularities produced by scattering are more interesting and realistic. Photo: David Neat

the paper copy is mounted onto a piece of thin card afterwards to keep it flat. An alternative, where only a flat carpet colour or very simple pattern is required, is provided by the adhesive velours found in hobby shops. The range of colours available is very limited, but white velour can be spray-painted. A simple stencil can be cut from stencil paper or etched in sheet metal to spray a basic repeat pattern. Alternatively, the paper layer peeled off Kapa-line foamboard can make a good carpet-like surface on its underside if enough is left intact. This will be easier to paint than velour and will even accept watercolour.

Scatter materials

There are common instances, such as when trying to convey a pebble beach or a gravel path, where the surface can only be successfully recreated by covering an area with glue and scattering something into it. Many scenic modellers prefer to create the effect of grass or soil in this way, which can be effective up to 1:50 scale. Model shops, particularly those catering for railway or terrain enthusiasts, will often stock a whole range of substances specially ground, chopped or dyed for the purpose – granulated cork, ground olive stones, dyed sawdust, fine grit or minced foam, to mention but a few. Pet shops are a good source for different kinds of sand and fine gravel used in aquariums, as well as sawdust. A look round the local supermarket will reveal other possibilities, for example poppy seeds, mixed herbs, dishwasher salt, coffee granules, ground nuts or cat litter!

If this method would seem the best or most interesting option there are some general points to be considered first. An obvious one perhaps is that if the material glued to the surface is the right colour to begin with and need not be painted, the base should approximate that colour because a lot of it will show through, however compactly covered. Then there is the choice of glue, which needs to be slow-drying, especially if covering a large area. Spray Mount keeps its tackiness for a while and may hold fine particles well, but larger granules will need to be better fixed. PVA is often used, but needs to be thinned a little so that it will cover better and even then it is preferable to do small sections at a time. Care must be taken to avoid overcovering the edges of previously completed areas, as this will create slight ridges that may spoil the effect wanted. For covering a large area in one go, a strong wallpaper paste may be a better option, or using a special glue designed for the purpose such as Hi-Tack, which is a very sticky and slow-drying form of PVA. Another alternative method of gluing, especially when using larger materials that may need to be arranged rather than scattered, is to mix them thoroughly with paint or PVA in a pot first and trowel them into place. PVA will dry to a somewhat shiny surface that may need to be worked on afterwards. Sometimes just sprinkling a material, particularly a large-grained one, into a bed of glue fails to produce the right effect because the particles just don't 'sit' together in the right way. In this instance, it may be better to arrange the material first and add the glue afterwards. PVA should be thinned to a watery consistency, adding a drop of washing-up liquid to help it flow. It can then be carefully dripped onto the surface and left to dry.

Some surfaces made by scattering materials into glue. The flat samples are, from left to right: coarse granulated cork, spray-painted sugar and aquarium grit. To the far right are saucers of vermiculite at the bottom and crushed eggshell above. The hedge form is made from a shaped piece of reticulated foam (large open cells) covered with poppy seeds and partially painted.

CHAPTER 7

PAINTING

Introduction

This chapter looks at the main options available for achieving primarily realistic finishes and effects in scale. Once again, because this book places emphasis on obtaining results using relatively uncomplicated means, techniques such as airbrushing or compressor-powered spray painting are not dealt with here. Working with these tools requires more information than can be contained in this book; there are many good ones to be found on the market. The product model-maker, most likely the one to rely on these and usually for less varied effects, may find some of the techniques culled from theatre and film work interesting, however, perhaps even suggesting some alternatives to standardized workshop practice.

The painting of models poses special problems, whatever the purpose. One is the consistency of paint used – the thinner the better, otherwise surface detail may be lost. Another is the variety of materials which need to be painted – it is hard to find a single paint type that will be equally suitable for all of them. Similarly, the variety of effects required can demand an arsenal of different methods. At such a small scale, brushwork may become either too fiddly or can look too mechanical and it may be that an effect can be better achieved by some form of 'controlled accident'.

Painting should never be left to the last minute! This may sound somewhat paradoxical, because often it can't come anywhere else in the process, but sufficient time should be set aside in order to do it properly. Models invariably take much longer than planned, even for the experienced model-maker, while deadlines, on the other hand, tend to remain stubbornly in place. The final stages of the process are therefore pushed into an ever tighter time frame, partly because one usually assumes that painting will be straightforward, or at least quick compared to everything else. The result is often that the final painting of important elements is crammed into the last day, with no room for experiment (or enjoyment!) and little chance either to respond positively or to cope calmly with the unforeseen. This may be the first opportunity one's really had to see the combined effect of each element in the colour that was, up to now, mainly envisioned in 'the mind's eye'. One has to have the freedom to be critical at such a point and the time to make any changes one feels are necessary.

In practice it can, and should, be possible. You should try to estimate long before how much time will probably be needed and add at least a full day to that. Having set that personal deadline it should be stuck to faithfully no matter what else happens. You can perhaps sell it to yourself as a much needed period of relative calm and relaxation – something to look forward to! Painting can become the most creative of the processes we have looked at. It is certainly more subject to mood and will suffer in a state of tension or pressure. This can be alleviated by a little planning, for example by having all foreseeable paints there when the time comes and a good stock of extra ones; having enough scraps of all materials used including offcuts of textures to make paint tests; and cleaning and tidying the workplace thoroughly beforehand and checking that the lighting conditions are optimal. Visual reference material should be properly organized and everything should be on-hand and visible while painting. If this is in the form of digital files, for example, it is worth printing the most relevant ones in good quality and tacking them to boards or the wall in front of you. There's nothing more irritating than having to locate or sort through folders of images while trying to concentrate on the act of painting.

Priming surfaces

Generally speaking, it is usually better to apply a basecoat to a surface to make it ready for painting. There are a number of reasons for this, but not all will apply in every case. In conventional painting a primer is necessary to seal a porous surface such as wood, canvas or plaster, because if paint is applied directly the solvent in the paint will be drawn away too quickly. This will affect the proper hardening of the paint, making it weak and flaky. The primer will also provide a better key for the paint whether the surface is porous or not, as is the case when painting plastic or metal. If a model element is made up from a number of different materials it makes sense to paint the whole

THE PROBLEM OF WARPING

Proper priming can also prevent a lot of grief or frustration when using water-based paints. Cardboard or thin wood will bend out of shape when painted directly with anything containing water. The amount of bending may vary according to the amount of water in the paint, but also the degree to which the binder in the paint shrinks as it dries. It may help somewhat to weight a flat piece down as soon as the surface is touch dry and wait for a day, but this is not always possible. Another solution would be to use oil- or spirit-based paints instead of water-based, or a third would be to rely on plastics rather than card or wood, although these solutions are rather limiting.

A better option would be to use either a spray primer or a non-water based wood primer to seal absorbent surfaces prior to painting. For example, a quick and effective universal primer can be found in any garage or shop that stocks car spray paints. Simoniz is the most common brand and this is available in white, mid-grey or red oxide (useful if you want a pre-coloured basecoat). Card may only need one fairly light spraying and should ideally be left to dry for a few hours before paint is applied over it. It is especially ideal for giving plastic or metal a smooth, paintable surface and will even accept thin washes. The disadvantage, as with any spray paint, is the effect it has on one's working atmosphere. Good ventilation is essential and ideally a space in the studio should be reserved for it (with an extractor fan, or it should at least be close to a window and partitioned off). Another note of caution is that these types of spray paint contain acetone as a solvent, which will dissolve styrofoam. Tests should be made on small pieces of material first. The alternative to this is to use a brushable, non-water-based primer. These are only marginally friendlier because they produce a lot of vapour and take longer to dry, but they can be thinned with white spirit and work out a lot cheaper.

As far as other methods of minimizing warping are concerned, another option which is sometimes effective is to paint the whole of the back of the card, or at least a generous cross shape, with the same paint to equalize the effects. In addition, painted card can be braced on the back if the base is still flexible enough. A final option might be to choose a thin paper to paint on, to let it buckle while drying, but then to spray-mount it onto a more stable construction.

thing in one basecoat colour first so that subsequent paint layers will behave the same throughout. Colour can be added to this basecoat, which will save both on the amount of paint needed and the time taken for the final coat. Even if not strictly needed, priming a surface will open up a greater range of painting methods. For example, the Kapa-line foam discussed as a surfacing material in the previous chapter, 'Creating Surfaces', will accept even ink or stainer but once there the colour cannot be rubbed down. Priming the surface will make it less absorbent so that thin colour can be dabbed off where required to preserve highlights.

Paint

One paint for all?

The answer is, most probably … no! There are so many different requirements and so many different ways of using or modifying paint that it is highly unlikely one will suit all. Faced with such an endless array, the natural tendency is to stick to a paint one understands and has a good stock of, using others only under special circumstances. Commercial model-makers tend to favour anything that can be sprayed, whereas theatre designers will usually attempt everything nowadays in tube acrylic.

An ideal paint for our varied purposes would have to be as follows: a paint that can be made thin enough not to clog fine detail, but which covers evenly without streaking; a paint that will dry totally matt, but which can be modified to produce anything between a semi-matt or gloss finish; a paint that will adhere to anything, but which can be removed with a harmless solvent; a paint that is cheap and readily available in at least all primary and secondary colours; a paint that can either be quick-drying or slowed down and that can be easily overpainted or used as a glaze … and so on! There isn't such a paint, but the main contenders useful to model-making are summarized here. More details on them are included in the paint section of the Directory of Materials.

Paint invariably consists of three main ingredients, whatever the type. There is the pigment, a finely ground powder which gives the paint its colour. A solvent is added to this to make it liquid, or rather to suspend the minute particles of pigment in a liquid. It could be used as it is at this stage, but would return to a powder once the solvent evaporates. The third ingredient is therefore a binder, an adhesive which binds the particles together and sticks them firmly to the surface. It is the last two ingredients, solvent and binder, which start to give the different paints their special properties. But there is often a fourth ingredient added, known as the filler, a colourless powder whose function is to thicken or extend the quantity of paint

Because the surface of this old façade has to remain as matt as possible a combination of airbrushing acrylics and matt enamel is being used. After both stone and brickwork have been given the same base colour, different areas are defined by dry-brushing colour on top. Individual bricks can be easily picked out on the surface pattern. Sharing a basecoat helps to unify the whole element.

without affecting the colour. It also makes the paint more opaque.

Acrylics

Acrylic paint comes closest of all to this ideal of a universal medium. It is water-based, mixes well and can be thinned. One can find it everywhere in a range of forms and prices. The difference between a cheap set of 'school' acrylics and the more expensive artists' range is mainly that the pigment is less finely ground in the cheaper paint and there will be more filler. The paint may not mix or thin so well and the colours could be dulled.

However, despite its versatility and the ease of working with it, acrylic paint isn't very 'model friendly' unless it is used with care. If used straight from the tube, for example, without taking the trouble to thin it evenly, it will clog and fill up fine detail, create brushwork textures where you don't want them and dry with an almost glossy but uneven finish. Some acrylics will even resist easy thinning, becoming stringy or glutinous, and making it difficult to paint a flat area without streaking. It can also be wasteful, because it dries too quickly on the palette. Far more acceptable for model-making are the more liquid acrylics sold in pots and sometimes specified for airbrushing (Americana from DecoArt is a fairly inexpensive range). These

tend to cover better and will dry with more of a matt finish. Although thinner, they, like standard tube acrylic, will adhere to plastic if the surface is keyed (rubbed lightly with fine sandpaper).

The rapid drying and self-sealing properties of acrylic can work to advantage. For example, even a thin wash can be relatively quickly overpainted without disturbing the colour underneath, making it ideal for dry-brushing or building up semi-transparent glazes, unlike watercolour or gouache. Both matting agents and retardants are available for most brands if a less silky finish or more working time is needed.

Gouache

Gouache is a form of watercolour to which a filler is added to make it more opaque. Like watercolour, it contains minimal binder, which means that it is not suitable for building up separate layers or glazes. If used to paint a figure that is going to be handled, for example, gouache will start flaking off fairly quickly unless it is sealed. Gouache is really only designed for painting on paper, but it covers well without streaking and will dry a satisfying matt. It changes tone as it dries, light colours becoming darker and dark colours generally a bit lighter. One use for it is for matting down elements that have turned out too shiny.

Making gouache into a more adhesive and durable paint by adding PVA. An equal amount of PVA to gouache is sufficient to increase its versatility without reducing its matt properties. The paint samples were painted on PVC which was very lightly sanded first.

Gouache's versatility can be greatly extended, however, by mixing in a binder such as PVA. If an equal ratio of PVA to paint is added it becomes far more durable and adherent and will even cover plastic, with the aid of light sanding beforehand. The filler will prevent the mixture from drying too 'silky', although adding a greater amount of PVA will make it progressively more so if this is needed. The result is a paint that has many of the properties of acrylic without some of the drawbacks and is well worth experimenting with.

Enamel paint

This may be familiar as the minuscule tins of paint dedicated to the painting of plastic aeroplane kits. Model shops are sure to stock them but they can also be found at some art shops. This paint should not be confused with traditional enamel, which needs to be baked at a high temperature to harden. It is an oil-based paint, needing white spirit to thin it or to clean brushes afterwards. The solvent evaporates fairly quickly in the air and the build-up of vapour can be unpleasant. Good ventilation is therefore essential when using this paint. Despite this drawback, enamel is one of the most 'model-friendly' paints in that it covers exceptionally well even when spread very thinly, with very little streaking. It can be painted on just about any surface without the need for priming and the surface is tough

and durable. It also dries very quickly and will make excellent washes or glazes. If heavily diluted with white spirit it can function very well as a stain. In terms of economy, the paint will keep for many years if the tin lid is properly closed because the oil rises to the top and acts as its own seal. For this reason, the paint needs to be thoroughly remixed if it has been sitting for some time.

Oil paint

It is not very common for model-makers to use oil paint, because oil paint takes so long to dry properly. Although the effects achievable with such a malleable medium could be beneficial and the colour range is excellent, the smell and the reliance on a spirit solvent are a distinct disadvantage. Also, in order to dry properly oil paint requires a suitably primed or sealed surface so that the oil is not sucked out too soon in the drying process.

Stains and inks

A variety of specially prepared wood stains can be found in most home-decorating centres to simulate a range of different woods. These are usually available in both water-based and

A page of samples showing different methods of staining: standard wood stain, liquid shoe polish and thinned enamel.

Detail of staining on obeche wood panelling. The stain brings out certain structures in the grain which are not previously visible. Once dry, a satin varnish gives an appropriate finish.

BELOW: Tree trunks may have elements of brown, but this is rarely the overall colour effect. Photo: David Neat

spirit-based form. On the whole, the spirit-based stains work better, penetrating the wood more thoroughly, with the added advantage that they will not warp a thin wood surface. However, these are quite expensive if only a little is needed and an acceptable alternative can be made by dissolving either a little oil pastel, powder pigment or even shoe polish in white spirit. A little can be added at first, the resulting colour tested and preferably left for a while, then more added if required. The examples of wood staining featured in Chapter 6, 'Creating Surfaces', were made with a mixture of white spirit and solid shoe polish. Alternatively, liquid shoe polish (sold in bottles with sponge applicators) produces an interesting result on wood or even cardboard. If left properly to dry, repeated coats will produce a darker and glossier effect (unlike conventional wood stain), saving the need for a separate varnish. A drawback is that this form of polish has a water base which may warp the material.

Anything which contains a pigment or dye (but no filler) can be tried as a stain, including inks. A handy source of concentrated ink is a spent inkjet printer cartridge, because there is usually an amount of ink left in the cartridge even when the printer programme has rejected it (apparently to save the system from drying out).

Cartridges can easily be prised open and the bag inside slit to drain out the ink. If experimenting with this ink it is worth putting a very small amount of PVA with it before colouring anything because otherwise it may not fix properly. The colours achievable can be very intense.

Even a contemporary brick surface shows many colour variations and an older brick wall will have more. Photos: David Neat

Techniques

Naturalism

We make assumptions about the colours of surfaces even if we are staring the real thing in the face. Take, for example, a manhole cover – because we know it to be made of metal, we automatically make the assumption that it should be modelled using a metal-like substance such as metal foil or the lead foil from wine bottle tops, which we would then emboss and darken to look like old metal. However, on closer inspection it will become apparent that an old manhole cover may have taken on the colour of the surrounding ground and, apart from its smoothness and patterning, could be modelled from the same stuff as used for the ground. It is easy to 'see' with the mind rather than the eyes. We fall victim to countless similar assumptions, many unchallenged since childhood – for example, skin is not pink, tree trunks are rarely brown and dirt is not black.

An ordinary brick wall, however simple it might appear to be, poses an exemplary painting challenge. Even a modern brick wall, where the bricks themselves are relatively uniform in composition and the structure has not yet been modified by the elements, is composed of a variety of colours and the more one looks, the more one will see.

The same is true of absolutes like black and white. Leaving the argument aside as to whether pure black or white even exist in nature or whether our senses could convey them, the fact is that many things we take to be pure black or white are not. Painters have long avoided using a straight black from the tube in favour of mixing two very dark opposing colours together (Prussian blue with burnt umber, pthalo green with alizarin crimson, for example) to represent more accurately the softer 'black' we are actually seeing. Since it is, in part, an attempt at an illusion, the model should be no different. Theatre designers often talk of a 'dirty black' to represent a black which looks more natural, more like a very dark tinted grey. Similarly, pure white would probably blind us if we ever saw it – and it certainly dazzles disastrously under theatre lighting. What we think of as white (a landscape of snow, for example) is more likely to be a very light blue or grey, even shades of pink. A photograph will reveal that to us, more than our eyes and minds do.

Representing reflective surfaces

Using actual gloss paint in a scale model has many drawbacks. Textural and painted effects should be just as subject to scale as built structures and high gloss usually tends to look out of scale. Reflective surfaces need to be very precise and gloss will show

LOOKING AT THE REAL THING

The Internet has already almost completely changed our methods of visual research and therefore our ways of seeing. It has made so much readily accessible to us, but certain things are lost in the process. For example, imagine that you decide to design and model a marble floor. You can Google the word 'marble' and an image search alone will give you hundreds of sample images detailing almost every type and colour of marble. You might even lift these, scale them down, print them off and paste them onto card. You might consider the job more or less done. You might have felt that, with this wealth of visual information at your fingertips, there was no need anymore to take the trouble to locate and look at an actual marble floor. However, you will almost certainly not have been given a true impression of how marble discolours with age, how and where it wears away, how prominent or subtle the joins can be. You won't have begun to see what this material actually looks like in a real, living space.

every minute imperfection in the surface. The paint usually needs a long time to dry, requiring a completely dust-free environment in the process. Unless the surface is properly primed, the result will be patchy. Once dry, the surface is difficult to modify or overpaint. Gloss paint tends to be thicker than other types and surface detail (such as scored lines between wall tiles, for example) may be lost. Unwanted brush marks are often visible and the choice of colours is also limited. The one advantage of gloss paint may be that the colour one sees in the tin is the colour that will remain when dry.

It is better to underplay glossy or polished surfaces, or at least to have the option of starting subtle and increasing if required. On the whole, it is better to paint as normal with your preferred medium and to use something like a varnish over that to bring it up to the desired surface quality. Tests need to be made to check how the tone or hue of a matt colour will change when varnished. Paints respond differently – gouache will change more than acrylic, for example. Also, when using varnishes not specifically intended for the underlying paint, tests need to be made to check compatibility. The varnish may dry cloudy or not dry properly at all. Using polish or wax instead of a liquid varnish, such as spraying with furniture polish or using shoe wax, can also be an option. Again, experiment first to check compatibility before ruining valuable work.

There are a number of effective alternatives to using paint to obtain a flat reflective surface. A glossy coloured paper or thin

Matt enamel paint was painted directly onto the sanded polyfilla surface of these forms. When dry, this was lightly sanded again to make some of the grain visible, then transparent shoe polish was rubbed in and buffed to give a subtle sheen.

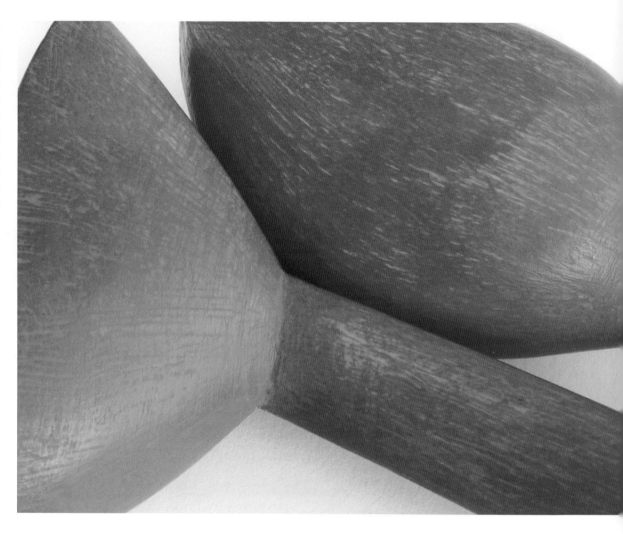

card such as Chromolux could be used to simulate ceramic tiling. Although the colour range is limited, precise tile divisions can be scored into it. Similarly, the glossy side of thin styrene could be used. Colours or effects can also be printed onto glossy photo paper. Sometimes applying self-adhesive film or spray-mounting acetate onto a coloured surface is an option, although this will always alter the colour. Another successful example might be the use of thin strips of Sellotape to represent lines of gloss against a matt colour.

The basecoat method

The derelict façade featured earlier was built up mainly in Kapa-line foam. This was primed with matt, water-based wall paint. In this case, the substructure was PVC so there was no danger of warping. It saved time to add colour directly to this rather than painting a coloured basecoat separately. Acrylic could be used to change the colour of the wall paint, but the special concentrated colourings or toners made for this purpose are more

effective. Applying the same basecoat colour to the whole structure helped to unify it, even if parts would eventually become different. A colour was chosen somewhere in the middle of the anticipated range, rather than the darkest or the lightest part. This gives the option of putting a dark wash on some parts where the paint will settle in the deeper lines and accentuate them and also to skim a lighter colour on top in places which will similarly pick up the brickwork pattern. Dark washes should be done very quickly with a full, soft brush so that there is time to dab paint away from the raised areas if need be. Using either a tissue, kitchen towel, fine sponge or cloth will produce a slightly different effect and should be experimented with.

This principle (starting with a mid-range basecoat and then modifying the colour either way on top of it) should be applied to almost any model painting task and will lead to more satisfying results. Often a flat, single colour will look dead, however interesting the texture might be. A more convincing and visually interesting result is obtained by creating the sense of an overall colour by the use of several different colours.

Detail of a façade. The unifying basecoat is visible underneath washes and overpainting.

Dry-brushing and highlighting

Dry-brushing is useful for accentuating a texture, for creating a worn or broken-down appearance, or for modifying a base colour without overpainting. Its effectiveness depends on the underlying texture, for example raised elements picking up the colour that is skimmed over them while recesses do not. This should be distinguished from dry-brushing effects onto a completely flat surface, which depends more on the character of the brush and the movement involved. To accentuate a textured or relief surface, the same colour can be used as the basecoat but made a little lighter.

When painting basecoats it is always a good idea to keep a small amount of each basecoat by for future use unless the colour mix is very simple and repeatable. It should be borne in mind, though, that just adding white to a colour to suggest the effect of light may simply dull the overall colour impression. This is most evident when using greens, for example with the painting of the tree in Chapter 4, 'Working with Metals'. Real leaves reflect light in an extraordinary way and a model tree can look so dead if the painting isn't varied to suggest this. Rather than just using white to lighten the green in this case, an equal amount of yellow should be included.

Always start subtle when dry-brushing, because it is easier to build up an effect rather than tone it down and a surface can quickly become too overworked or 'busy'. The best brushes to use for dry-brushing at model scale should be soft but rigid – for example, synthetic acrylic brushes are good for this purpose, whereas hogshair brushes are too unyielding while watercolour brushes yield too much. The shape of the brush is also important, with a medium flat one working better than a thin round one. The brush is better used on the flat (like rubbing with a crayon), rather than on its point.

A lot will depend on how you personally use brushes, so it's best to experiment first. Put a small amount of paint on the brush and take this to your palette or a non-absorbent surface. Offcuts of PVC are useful for this. Spread the paint evenly all over the brush. Dry-brushing a surface at this stage will produce a bold but blotchy effect. Unless that's what you want it's better to take a tissue and wipe a lot of the paint off. Then roll the brush around on the palette surface to distribute the paint once again. Dry-brushing is best done very lightly, just skimming the surface. Wait for the first effects to dry properly before deciding whether to go further. This is because paints, especially gouache, can dry lighter or darker depending upon their composition. Although a good brush is by far the best tool for dry-brushing, sponges, rag or tissues can also be effective by wetting with the minimum amount of paint and dabbing on the surface.

Detail of rocks. After the basecoat, lighter colours were skimmed on using the flat of a soft brush to bring out the texture. To complete the effect speckles were flicked on using a hogshair or toothbrush.

Details of subtle dry-brushing effects on model furniture. The quilt was suggested using the pattern on a piece of kitchen towel spray-mounted onto aluminium foil so that it could be shaped. After painting a base colour the pattern needed to be emphasized.

Subtle dry-brushing can be very effective for suggesting a worn appearance, such as on the leather sofa shown in the photo, because the paint will naturally settle on those raised areas more likely to be worn. For similar reasons it can enhance the look of model draperies, especially in creating the look of velvet or satin curtains, because it introduces an element of 'sheen' in the appropriate places. Sheen is different here from glossiness. Applying a gloss coat for this effect would just make the curtains look wet. For a true velvet effect, however, it is necessary to take a step first in the opposite direction because deeper folds need to be darkened first. The only way to do this is to paint or spray the whole thing darker and bring the colour back by dry-brushing over the top.

Although oil paint should be used with caution, it does have an advantage in this context because it remains workable for much longer and can be softened or removed almost completely if mistakes are made. Darker colours are also more trans-parent. It should be done as a last step (and then only if the surface is already sealed with paint and it can be left to dry for days afterwards), because it is not compatible with other paints if the surface needs further treatment.

Rubbing a paste colour on is a form of dry-brushing. An effective gold used in picture framing and theatre prop work is Finger Gold. It is like a polish but contains gold-like powder in suspension. It can be rubbed onto a surface (the darker the bet-ter), usually with the finger, left a little to dry and then buffed to a shine. The buffing flattens the minute gold particles against the surface, hence they reflect more.

Alternatively, it is worth experimenting with pastels in a similar way, putting a little pastel on the tip of a finger and rub-bing onto raised areas. This will stay well enough if the model piece isn't going to be handled too much. Coloured pencils can also be rubbed directly onto the painted surface, although the softer the brand of pencil, the better.

The cast decorative frieze from Chapter 3 has been given a basecoat of matt enamel. Finger Gold has then been rubbed onto the raised pattern. A cotton bud is a good alternative to the finger for more detailed work.

Distressing the paint surface

This comical term is used mainly in theatre and film to describe the action of breaking down a new-looking surface to make it look old or worn. As has been shown, dry-brushing or rubbing in lighter colours is often sufficient to convey wear or decay on a small scale, but it is useful to know what could be achieved by other means. This includes mechanical abrasion (that is, attacking the surface with sandpaper or tools), using a solvent to dissolve the paint, or preparing the surface prior to painting to produce a certain effect. As for the first, the effects will be different depending upon the grade of sandpaper, the type of paint and the material painted. There are no helpful generalizations to be made; it's a matter of individual testing. Wire brushes (the kind sold for brushing suede shoes) or steel wool may produce better results because they can reach parts that sandpaper can't.

Similarly, the effects of solvents are too various to mention them all. Acetone, for example, is a powerful solvent on most spray paint. Whereas water or white spirit may be effective in combination with deliberate rubbing for removing certain other paints, acetone is immediately effective on contact. If dripped from a pipette onto a spray-painted surface, for example, acetone can break up the paint to form patterns. When the acetone has evaporated, these patterns will remain on the surface. Unfortunately, there is no guarantee as to the exact effect, as it will depend upon the type of spray paint used.

Sgraffito

The word 'sgraffito' comes from the Italian and means 'to scratch'. In painting it usually implies scratching into paint while painting, or before it has dried. For the examples shown

139

Examples of sgraffito using gouache/PVA on plastic.

here, gouache was mixed with PVA glue and painted onto lightly sanded PVC. The effect at the top left was achieved by scratching with the other end of the brush while the paint was still wet, while the other samples were left to dry before a scalpel blade was used. Depending upon whether the paint is totally dry and the angle at which the blade is held, either coarse or finer scratches can be made. Wire brush or sandpaper could also be used for this. The technique depends on the paint sitting on the surface rather than being absorbed into it, so surfaces such as PVC or oil-painting paper are most suitable.

Craquelure

This is the term given to the minute surface cracking on old oil paintings or pottery glazes. When it occurs with paint it is usually the result either of two surfaces (that is, undercoat and topcoat) drying at different rates, or something that has been added to the paint itself. It is very difficult to simulate minutely the real-scale peeling of paint that has been exposed to the elements, so forcing a craquelure effect may be an option. One has to be careful, though, because even if it works it might be totally the wrong scale. As mentioned before, one has to develop a sense of what liberties are justifiable to suggest the 'essence of the look', or to convey one's own stylistic intentions, as opposed to being simply inaccurate or misleading.

A special agent, often termed a 'cracking' medium, is available from hobby or art suppliers. For the examples shown a basecoat was first applied to PVC. The thinner acrylics work best for this, though a spray primer or enamel could also be used. It actually doesn't matter what the basecoat consists of, but when dry it should be fairly generously covered with an even layer of the cracking medium, which is then left until it is touch dry. A second layer of acrylic, in a contrasting colour to the first, is then carefully brushed onto this surface. It helps to use a soft flat brush and a flowing paint mixture. Here, it does matter what type of paint is used; usually an opaque water-based paint is the most effective. Almost immediately, this top coat of paint will start separating as it dries, exposing the colour underneath. It may need a few hours to dry completely. The direction of the cracks will tend to follow the brushstrokes used, hence the slight differences in these samples.

Weathering, dirtying-down and tinting

Sometimes it is necessary to be especially subtle, for example if one is trying to recreate the effect of an old interior wall where

Examples of craquelure using a special 'cracking' medium between coats of acrylic. Different brushstrokes will result in slightly different patterns.

Tinting surfaces with coloured pencil dissolved in white spirit.

the outlines of past paintings or furniture reveal the ageing of the surface. Or take the sometimes very gradual build-up of dirt starting at the base of an outside wall. For these purposes paint may be too brutal, or at least too difficult to control. Putting a little pastel crayon on a finger or cloth and gently rubbing may be one solution, but here is a little known technique that may be more effective and suggest other painting applications.

Most people are familiar with watercolour or 'aquarelle' pencils that are soluble in water and can be used either on wetted paper or in conjunction with brushes to produce effects. What is not so well known is that most ordinary colouring pencils can be used in a similar way, if white spirit is used instead of water. This technique relies on the painting surface being, at the most, only slightly absorbent – oil-painting paper, or a surface primed with Simoniz spray or a spirit-based primer are ideal for this. It

also helps greatly if the surface is a little rough to begin with, so that when a coloured pencil is rubbed against it a suitable amount of pigment is transferred. For the samples shown here (which have been exaggerated for ease of viewing; much subtler effects are possible), polyfilla textures were rubbed along one edge with coloured pencil. A dab of white spirit was put onto a strong tissue or piece of soft cloth and this was rubbed over the pencil pigment. The pigment immediately dissolves, producing a stronger colour which was worked slowly into the surface. The technique needs to be practised, but continued rubbing will spread the colour and the effect will become subtler as one moves along. At any stage the pigment can be removed with more white spirit if the surface is suitably semi-absorbent to begin with. Being able to paint on and rub off easily in this way means that one has a greater control than one usually obtains with 'liquid' paints.

If used for direct painting, for example on oil-painting paper, the technique can be used for subtle gradations of colour, as shown in the second example. If the right kind of coloured pencil is used (that is, with a good pigment content), the colours can be quite rich. When the surface is dry, effects can also be created by rubbing the paint off with an ordinary eraser.

Masking out/using stencils

This is usually only applicable when working with sprays because the action of brushing often disturbs whatever barrier is used for masking, but if carefully done the following can be achieved by both masking out and using stencils.

For a hard, straight edge between two colours painters will often use masking tape, which is an inexpensive, low-tack paper tape. If you do this a lot it is a good idea to keep a roll reserved just for this purpose and store it in a polythene bag because in general use the roll will get a 'furry' edge in time and this will affect the sharpness of your painted edge. Although masking tape is designed to be pulled off most surfaces without damaging them, it may still affect delicate

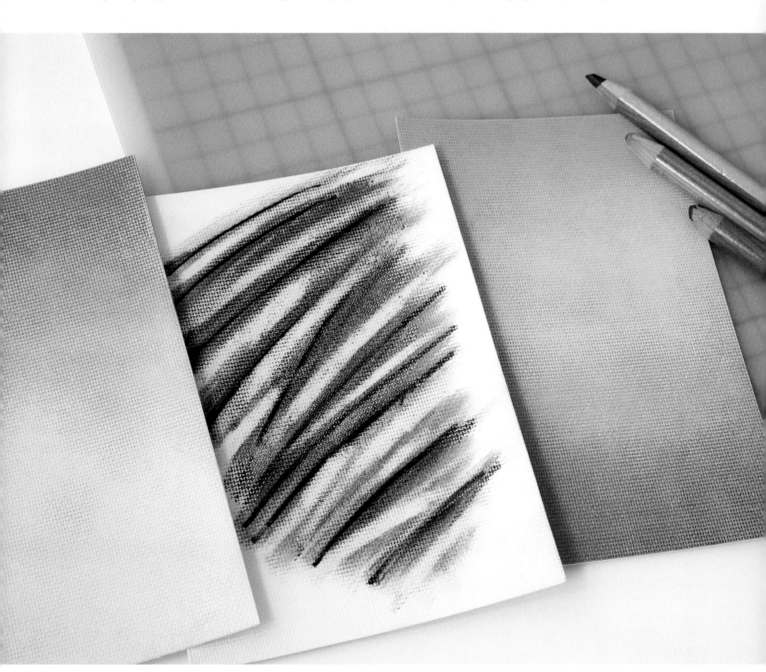

Effects produced with pencil and white spirit on oil-painting paper.

Using masking tape to paint straight lines. The tape is applied over the strip to be painted and then cut to fit the line.

Spraying a tile effect using a simple pattern cut in stencil paper. The edges can become slightly blurred if the stencil is not completely flat on the paper, or if the paint is sprayed from any direction other than directly above. Coins were used to weight the stencil flat. It helps to emphasize the divisions between the tiles afterwards.

surfaces. It can be made even less tacky by pressing on clothing or a cutting mat once or twice. However, the less it sticks the more likely paint will creep underneath the edge while painting. It may be best to re-cut the edge of the tape on a cutting mat to clean it up again before sticking it in place. The bone or plastic spatulas used in bookbinding are perfect for smoothing the edge of the tape down; otherwise use the back of a fingernail.

Where possible, a better method is to lay the tape down so that it overlaps the edge you want to paint and re-cut on that line, peeling the excess away. It can be difficult to put tape down in a perfectly straight line otherwise. Re-cutting on the

work is certainly the best method if a long thin strip will be painted, where two cuts are made along the centre of the tape and this strip is then peeled away.

For painting, a soft brush should be used and paint should be brushed over and away from the edge rather than towards it. The type of paint will make a big difference here. If it is too thin, like ink, it will absorb quickly into the paper and bleed under the edge of the tape however careful you are. If it is too thick, on the other hand, it will form a skin over the taped edge which may create a jagged break when the tape is pulled off. The thinner form of acrylic is a suitable paint here, but enamel paint will work even better.

Masking film: this is designed mainly for airbrush spraying and may not withstand the action of a brush. It can usually be cut, using a very sharp blade point, without significantly cutting into what's underneath. It will stick well to plastic, but in this case it's better not to sand the plastic first. Generally, the smoother the surface the better it will stick.

Masking fluid: this is basically latex. It is stocked in art shops mainly for watercolourists wishing to isolate a controlled area of white paper before laying down a wash. It will mask better than masking film when using inks or thin washes, but its main advantage is in enabling fluid forms or spots because shapes are painted on rather than cut. It is difficult to apply to plastic unless the surface is first keyed by light sanding.

Stencils: these are useful if a simple form has to be repeated. If the scale allows it, stencilling may be a quick way of suggesting a wallpaper pattern unless it's possible to print it. In the case of carpet patterns painted on fabric or velour it may be the only satisfactory and quick way. Thin styrene (such as 0.25mm) is

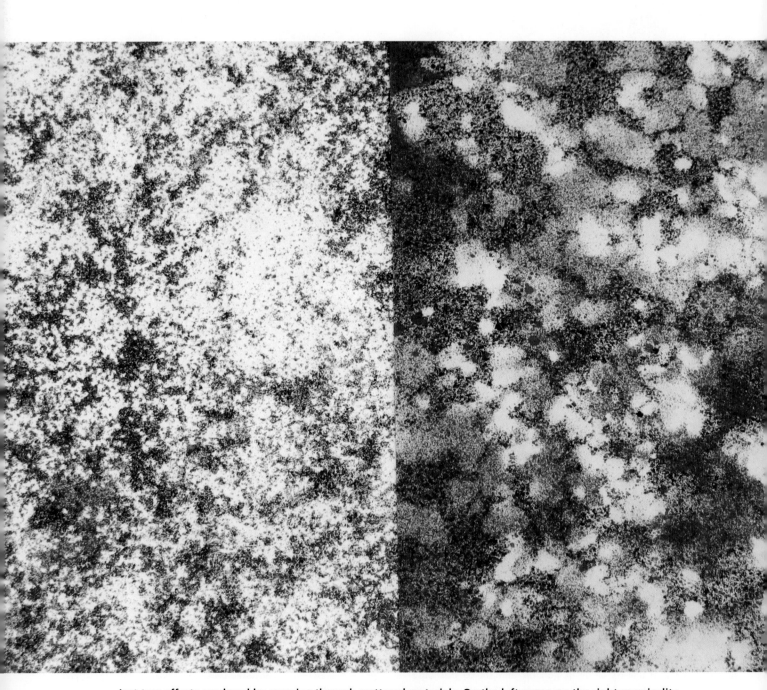

Just two effects produced by spraying through scattered materials. On the left sugar, on the right vermiculite.

Dick Bird's set model for *The Gambler* (Opera Zuid, Maastricht), showing the very effective
use of a photographic image to represent marble. Photo: David Neat

ideal as a stencil material. It will hold its shape and can be
washed carefully. Stencil paper is designed for large-scale work
and may be too thick for minute details. A better method,
achieving seriously intricate detail, may be to etch in thin metal
as described in Chapter 4, 'Working with Metals'.

Using spray paint

The main advantages of spraying a colour on as opposed to
brushing are that it is generally quicker and easier to achieve a
smooth and even coverage (*see* the example in Chapter 6,

'Creating Surfaces'). It may be the only option when stencilling
an effect as shown on page 145. The disadvantages are that
spray cans are expensive, much of the paint is wasted and one's
breathing space is quickly filled with paint and solvent. Spray
paints come in various forms including those with an acrylic,
enamel or cellulose base. In most cases, tests need to be made
first because those which contain acetone as a solvent will dissolve the surfaces of plastic. Another form of stencilling or
masking is shown opposite. To create these paint effects, sugar
was sprinkled onto paper and lightly sprayed through. The
sugar was then removed, re-sprinkled and sprayed through
with another colour. The same was done with larger particles of

vermiculite. Different effects can be achieved in the same way using, for example, open-weave fabrics or mesh, breakfast cereal, beads or confetti!

Painting with the computer

Nowadays, almost anyone involved in any aspect of the field of visual creation will need the whole kit: computer, colour printer, scanner and digital camera. The choice of software to accommodate particular needs may not be as definite, but the majority will have an image manipulation program such as Photoshop or Paint Shop Pro.

I mentioned above the example of creating a convincing marble floor by lifting colour samples from the Internet and printing them on satin or glossy photo paper. There was also the example in the previous chapter of printing out a carpet pattern at low resolution to keep it 'fuzzy'. There are countless other ways of manipulating photographic material, colour and form to create inkjet 'painted' surfaces and here is just one of the more usual ones.

Creating custom-scale wallpaper

The procedure couldn't be easier, although it relies on having a reasonably good and versatile printer to hand and, as mentioned, a digital program you're familiar with. Here, Paint Shop Pro is used, but the steps using Photoshop will be similar. First find some well-defined pattern on the net, or scan at medium resolution from a good photographic source, such as a book on William Morris for example. Obviously copyright may be an issue and it should be taken seriously! If in doubt, it is always better to get permission. Publishers or other companies are usually satisfied if something is used for the development of a design rather than faithfully copied. A better alternative might be, as I have done here, to adapt or create your own pattern along similar lines.

Open this image (whether borrowed or created) in Paint Shop Pro and use the crop tool to adjust or isolate the portion you want to use for a pattern, visualizing how it might look when repeated. I usually prefer to work to an equal-sided square because it makes calculations a little easier later, but it doesn't have to be. If you have a rectangle but want to make it into a square without cropping anything you can alter its proportions using the 'resize' tool. Go to 'Image' then 'Resize' and in the dialogue box that opens, enter the same number of pixels for height and width. Before this, you have to remember to uncheck the 'Lock Aspect Ratio' box at the bottom. Click on 'OK' to make the change. This will stretch the image to fit and it's a good tool to

remember when manipulating found images for use on a scale model!

It can be difficult sometimes, but also interesting, deciding how to crop an image to ensure a believable, workable pattern. But if you go straight to a wallpaper retailer's website you don't have to do any of that! Open the largest sample image of a wallpaper of your choice (they will usually have a good range of period styles, or at least reproductions that will serve), right-click on the image to bring up a menu, click on 'Save Background As', and file it away. When you open the image later it will be in a repeatable format, because you've saved the individual tile that the larger image was composed of. You can find and isolate individual tiles everywhere on the net by using this method.

Whether you find, paint and scan, or digitally generate your own tile, it's always better to start with a reasonable size even though it's going to become much smaller. When reducing it, the program will fit as much detail as possible into the reduction. If you start with a tiny image which then has to be enlarged even slightly, the loss of clarity might be noticeable. On the other hand, if you have a piece of pattern with too much detail in it and find you have to enlarge it to make it work, you can only enlarge the scale up to 250 per cent with this particular program.

What you need to do then is to save your image in the Paint Shop Pro 'Patterns' folder. This means it can be quickly accessed by the tool you'll be using later on. Click on 'File' then 'Save As' and find Paint Shop Pro in the browser, then find its 'Patterns' folder. Save directly to this folder. Think about the title you give it because when you open the 'Patterns' folder later there are lots of stock patterns already there, arranged alphabetically by file title, amongst which you will need to find your pattern.

When you've saved to 'Patterns' you can dismiss the file for the moment. Now you have to open a new file to create the pattern in the size you want. Again go to 'File' and click on 'New'. A dialogue box entitled 'New Image' will open. Either choose a preset image size (for example, if you just want a full A4 sheet of wallpaper pattern use the preset '8 × 10in vertical', which is near enough A4), or enter the dimensions of what you want printed out in centimetres. It would be a good idea here to enter an image height which corresponds to the height of the part of the model wall which will be covered in wallpaper. For example, if you are covering 3m walls from bottom to top, enter an image height of 12cm (3m at 1:25, if you are working in that scale). It's better to do this at this stage so that you can judge the scale of what will come up on the computer screen later.

Having entered the dimensions, click on the 'Color' preview field at the bottom. This will open up the all-important 'Materials' window. Click on 'Pattern'. Make sure that you uncheck 'Texture' on the right (unless you particularly want a wallpaper design with a textural effect superimposed).

Activate the drop-down menu on the active sample window to the left and find your tile amongst the collected patterns there. Click on it; you will return to the previous 'Materials' window, but your pattern will now appear as the active material.

You have the option of changing the scale with the slider on the right, but for the moment leave the scale at 100 per cent and click 'OK'. Having received an idea of how the pattern will look at this percentage, making it larger or smaller in scale is just a matter of repeating the process with a different percentage entered.

You will notice that the block of pattern you've produced is near, but not quite, the size it will be printed (the dimensions you had specified). If you want a more exact view to judge how the pattern will look, go to 'View' and select 'Palettes', then 'Overview'. This little thing will allow you to adjust the size of the screen image in single percentages until it measures up to the dimensions you initially entered (this only changes the viewing size; it doesn't change the printing size). Make a note of what percentage you've arrived at because you may need to establish it again later.

Now all you need to do is adjust the scale of the pattern if necessary (in the 'Material' window, where you were earlier), save it just in case and print out what you need.

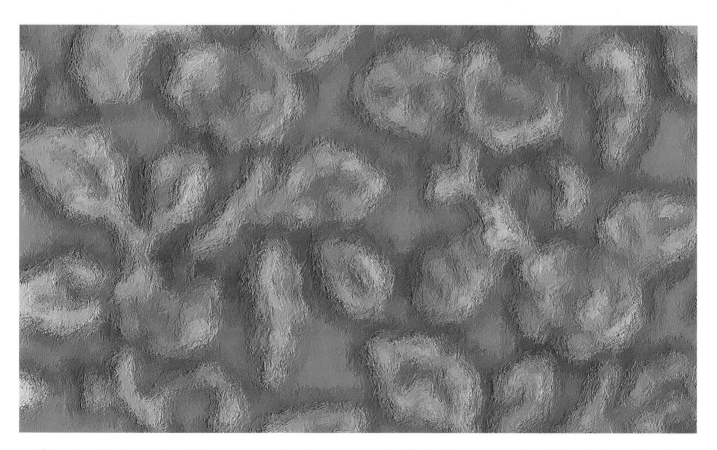

This pattern has been adapted from a source, altered to create a softer 'flocked' appearance, then tiled and adjusted in scale.

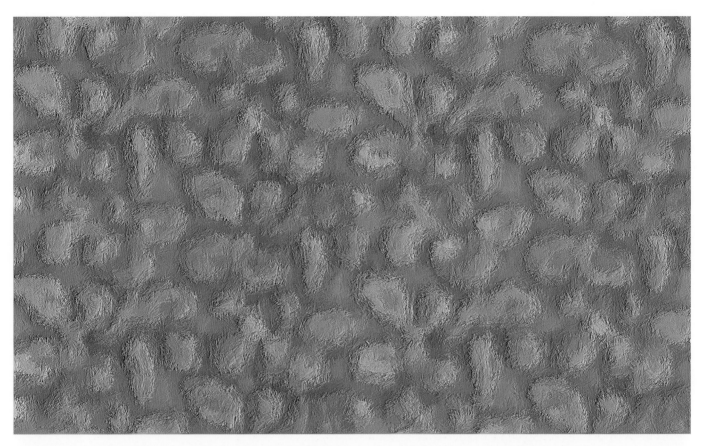

One must bear in mind that both 'texture' and colour balance will change with the scale.

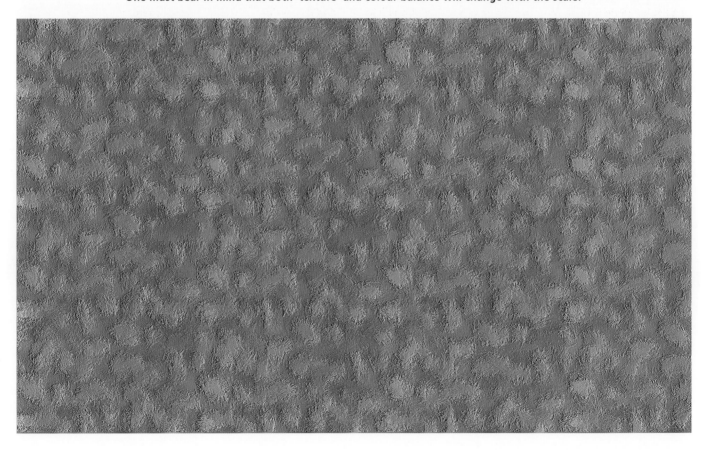

DIRECTORY OF MATERIALS

Materials for construction

Plastics

PVC

This is a particularly versatile and workable plastic, used extensively in architectural model-making. The type featured almost exclusively in this book is more properly termed 'foamed PVC' and goes by the brand names Foamex, Forex or Foamalux, depending upon where it comes from. The initials PVC stand for polyvinyl chloride. Foamed PVC is obtainable from specialist suppliers of plastics, shops selling display materials and some model shops. Price varies according to thickness and brand, but an 8ft × 4ft sheet of the thinnest (1mm), for example, averages at £13. It can be used in place of card for any form of building and is especially suited for finely detailed cutting. It can be embossed or scored lightly as a surfacing material, or used as a waterproof material for mould boxes.

Foamed PVC is most commonly stocked in pure white, but a range of colours is available. It also comes in many thicknesses, from 1mm to as much as 18mm. It consists of a smooth, slightly shiny outer surface with a less dense interior; hence it is very light for something so relatively strong. It is so easy to cut that even 10mm plastic can be managed eventually, cutting from both sides with a scalpel (and certainly with a Stanley knife). Edges can be sanded to a sharp finish with no fuzzing (unlike cardboard). It can be carved, but if the interior is exposed the surface will be slightly porous and 'pithy' and will need to be filled if any smoothness is required. Being a plastic, it is unaffected by humidity and will not absorb water. It is also unaffected by a number of solvents, including white spirit and acetone. This material is particularly resistant to any form of warping, even if left out in the sun. This rigidity is mainly due to its layered composition, acting like a cross-strutted girder. Thinner sheets can be bent into smooth curves but need to be firmly glued in place (top and bottom), otherwise they will revert.

Because cut edges are slightly porous, gluing works perfectly with cyanoacrylate (superglue), producing a virtually unbreakable bond. But if mistakes are made there is a special 'debonder' that you can buy for superglue which softens it and allows you to take the materials apart. If you can get hold of pure acetone (often from a good pharmacy) this will work just as well.

If PVC is given a spray coat of Simoniz primer even thin paints can be used to paint it. It won't absorb like soft card so some watercolour effects are out, but if these are desired then it is simple enough to spray-mount watercolour paper onto it.

Styrene

This is a versatile plastic available in many forms. It is ideal as a constructional material for particularly fine or delicate forms and its bending properties make it more suitable for curved elements. It can be found in suppliers of plastics and some model shops and is relatively cheap.

This is polystyrene, similar to the more familiar white packaging material but unexpanded in this case and usually referred to as just styrene to differentiate it.

It is harder to cut than PVC, because it is denser, but it is available in thicknesses down to 0.13mm, which is translucently thin. Thicknesses up to 1mm can still be cut with a knife fairly easily, but foamed PVC is a better option in this case. Its slight brittleness (compared to foamed PVC) can be used to advantage because it can be scored and snapped for a clean break. Often the surface will be matt on one side and glossier on the other. White is most common, but it is also available in black and a range of colours. It is also available in a seemingly infinite variety of rods, tubes, strips and sections (for example, 'L', 'H' and 'T' sections) and also a clear sheet version which is softer but less crystal clear than acetate.

Styrene bonds well with superglue, although if the styrene is very thin the glue will make it buckle. For a cleaner form of gluing there is a special solvent designed for styrene which effectively melts the two surfaces together. Since this solvent is water-thin, it can be brushed into a joint while the two parts are held in place and bonding happens almost immediately. This is a definite advantage when one has to glue a long curved strip, for example, doing it in carefully positioned stages and where it is difficult to apply glue to the whole strip at once. Styrene is much more bendable than foamed PVC, especially if heat is used to form a shape. For this reason, it is commonly used in vacuum forming.

ABS

This is a tougher form of styrene, often found in model shops as preformed strips and shapes. These can be useful for stronger, load-bearing construction, or as an alternative to PVC or styrene where more heat-resistance might be needed, for example under hot lights.

ABS is short for acrylonitrile butadiene styrene. It is the plastic that most people think of as plastic and is the stuff of computer housings, mobile phones and so on. It is tough, although its hardness varies with the make, and it is heat resistant. Consequently, it's not so effective as a model material because it is less easy to cut or shape, while durability in model-making isn't necessarily a major issue. It can be glued most effectively with superglue or plastic solvent.

Acetate

This is a thin, glass-clear sheet plastic which can be found in model shops, art and graphics suppliers or photocopy shops. An A4 sheet can cost as little as £0.20, depending upon the thickness. It is useful to represent glass in model windows, to suggest the surface of water, or (when photocopied or inkjet printed) to represent gauzes, fine mesh or translucent curtains. Acetate intended for printing is treated on one side to accept ink, which gives it a slightly grainy appearance.

A favourite for model window panes, acetate does the job well as long as the right thickness is chosen for the size. For anything bigger than 5 × 5cm square in the model it is best to use a 0.5 thickness, for example. Superglue (applied very carefully via the end of a cocktail stick and then only in strategic spots) is the best for gluing it. But this brings another drawback. Unless it's very minimally dosed, the fumes from the superglue will 'fog' the acetate in places. Either one has to be very careful, or apply a coat of clear varnish to the acetate afterwards which should eliminate much of the fogging. As an alternative, you could use slivers of double-sided tape to attach the acetate to the frame. These will hold well enough even for a permanent model under normal conditions.

There are alternatives to acetate for building transparent constructions, for example clear styrene, clear PVC and HIPS (high-impact polystyrene). Not quite as crystal-clear as acetate, they're much softer and gluing is apparently easier. They may be less likely to 'fog' than acetate, as well as being less brittle and easier to cut. For more rigid, see-through constructions, acrylic glass is more suitable, usually available in thicknesses upwards from 1mm. A special solvent or clear glue is necessary for bonding parts together cleanly.

Polypropylene

This can be found in 'frosted' sheet form (usually in 0.5mm or 1mm thicknesses) in graphics suppliers, model and hobby shops. It is particularly useful for representing frosted glass, large flat gauzes or BP (back projection) screens in a model. It is flexible and will cut easily and cleanly with a knife. The surface is extremely slippery, so it is advisable either to lay tape down and cut through that or use a good non-slip ruler. Polypropylene poses a problem to glue and even superglue will not take well to it. The best options are either to slot it into some form of supporting structure without gluing, or, when used to convey frosted windows, to tack it with thin strips of double-sided tape where these can be hidden. 1mm polypropylene is rigid enough to stand up on its own without requiring much support and may only need to be held in place at the sides. A range of colours is usually available and these can be quite rich even though the surface is frosted.

Foam

Styrofoam

Styrofoam is a rigid foam which is ideal for carving and sanding, being a fine-celled, extruded version of polystyrene. It has long been popular in film and theatre workshops even for fairly detailed decorative work (in the UK, styrofoam refers to the finer, blue material rather than the more common white packaging material). It can be bought from builders' merchants (because it is manufactured as an insulation material), but is also available in other thicknesses from good model or hobby shops. The average price for a 600 × 1,200mm sheet of 25mm blue styrofoam, for example, is £20 (this is the form it commonly comes in at builders' merchants). It is extremely useful: as a constructional material for thick forms; as a shaping material which can be easily carved, sanded (for example, for rocks and landscapes); or as thin sheet which can be textured and used as surfacing.

This highly versatile form-making material comes in different colour versions, which differ from each other mainly in density. The blue type, also referred to sometimes as Roofmate from an earlier brand name, is the most common. The pink type is slightly denser and sands to a finer finish, while the white variety is denser and finer still. This is quite expensive compared to the standard blue. Styrofoam is properly named 'extruded polystyrene' as opposed to the common 'expanded poly-styrene' used as packaging. Its cells are much smaller, therefore it is denser and more robust than the expanded type.

Styrofoam is very easy to cut with a knife and to sand because of its rigidity. Once smooth, the surface can be coated with polyfilla or similar, and this can then be sanded to an eggshell finish if required. If the covering is combined with a mesh or fabric (as with fibreglass resin and matting), it results in a very strong, durable form. But resin will dissolve the surface of styrofoam (as will epoxy fillers, most spray paints and many glues), so before laminating in fibreglass the form's surface needs to be thoroughly sealed with a water-based filler. Shellac, a natural sealant, will also do this well.

The best glues to use are water-based, for example PVA will glue styrofoam if the surfaces to be glued are flush. If not, it may be better to use something like polyfilla or a gap-filling adhesive. Scenic workshops favour using a two-part expanding polyurethane foam to bond pieces together where a greater amount of gap-filling is required. The advantage of this is that the bond ends up much the same consistency as the styrofoam, making carving much easier.

Polyurethane foam

For the qualities of the special type of polyurethane foam found in Kapa-line foamboard look under 'Card' below (in addition to Chapter 2). Other forms of rigid polyurethane foam are in common use and come in sheets with a variety of densities. Some tend to be very crumbly and unpleasant to work with, while others are so dense they can only be shaped with machine tools. Extra care needs to be taken when sanding these types of polyurethane foam because the dust is abrasive and shouldn't be breathed in or get into the eyes!

Plastazote

This is a flexible, rubber-like sheet foam produced in a wide variety of thicknesses, densities and colours. It can usually only be obtained from specialist suppliers of foam rubber, but hobby shops commonly stock small and colourful sheets of a thinner, finer version. It is useful as a constructional material for lightweight, flexible forms, but can also be used to clad sur-faces. It slices well with the knife but cannot be sanded. For glu-ing, a synthetic rubber contact adhesive such as Evo-Stik Impact is recommended. This can provide a very tough bond that is even effective for piecing sections together edge to edge. Superglue can work very well with the thinner 'hobby'

versions. Plastazote is resistant to many things, certainly water. It contracts with heat and will do so very quickly under the heat gun. It will respond to a certain amount of heat-bending in this way.

Reticulated foams

One of these is featured as a useful material for making foliage, illustrated in Chapter 4. These foams are composed of a net-work of filaments, which are all that remains of the bubbles formed during the foaming process. They are manufactured principally as industrial filters. Sheets (in various cell sizes) can be found in good model shops, especially those catering for architectural model-making. The foam is a favourite for making small-scale trees.

Metal

Sheet metal

Small, thin sheets of brass, copper or aluminium can be com-monly found in model shops. Cutting these is relatively easy by scoring with a knife and then bending (although copper will need more bending). Buying brass sheet in the form of sculptor's shim is more economical, averaging £5 for a 160mm × 2.5m roll. This is normally 0.1mm thickness and is suitable for the work illustrated in Chapter 4. If used as cladding, Spray Mount or double-sided tape can work for gluing (although the surface needs to be thoroughly cleaned and keyed first using wire wool). Otherwise, use a stronger contact adhesive. The thin aluminium foil from food containers is a good source for cladding small areas.

Rods

This is available in a range of solid sections and tubes, whether round or square. Brass is the most convenient metal for solder-ing. Rods up to a certain thickness can be easily cut with a scalpel by scoring and breaking. Aluminium is usually available in larger gauges but this is not as easy to solder.

Piano wire

This is a fine, hard wire sold in straight lengths. Being steel, it keeps its shape well but can be bent using pliers if needed. Piano wire is most useful for hanging elements in a model, more precise than thread or nylon.

Aluminium wire and florist's wire

The most versatile form of wire is aluminium because it is very soft. Sculptors prefer it for the creation of armatures and a good sculpture supplier will sell a variety of thicknesses. It will also endure repeated bending, which is why it's commonly used for stop-motion puppet armatures. So-called 'florist's wire' is similarly soft and workable, if thinner wire is needed.

Metal mesh

Various sizes can be found, ranging from fine 'impression mesh' (usually copper or aluminium), which is punched, to larger-scale welded wire mesh. Impression mesh can be moulded to an extent because the holes will expand or contract. The finer varieties can be used for creating rigid curtains, while the larger are commonly used as bases for terrain modelling. Welded wire mesh is not mouldable in the same way, but has other special uses which are illustrated in Chapter 4.

Wood

It is becoming less common for either the freelance or the occasional model-maker to use wood as a constructional material, despite its heritage, because it demands more of an equipped workshop set-up. Also, good-quality, thin sheet wood is generally more expensive than the alternatives, or is harder to obtain. An exception might be made sometimes in the case of architectural models, where a clean wood surface may be valued for its aesthetic qualities. But even here it is common to construct first in plastic and apply the wood as a finishing layer. The other exception is where a firm, solid material is needed as a baseboard. More about woods such as obeche, balsa and walnut has been included in the section of the Directory dealing with surfaces.

MDF

This is a processed form of wood composed of tightly pressed fibres bound together with glue. The initials stand for 'medium density fibreboard'. It is easily obtainable from builders' or timber merchants, or DIY centres. Good model shops may stock thinner types down to 2mm. It has its advantages as a cheap constructional material which can be easily glued using PVA wood glue. It is commonly used for baseboards because it maintains its flatness better than plywood, but these can get very heavy.

Wood strip and dowel

Model shops will stock a wide variety of strips and dowels (round section) in various thicknesses while DIY centres will offer larger sizes. The light-coloured woods in model shops will tend to be bass, obeche, spruce or pine, while the harder, darker wood is usually walnut. DIY centres will often stock strip and dowel in pine or ramin. Ramin is slightly harder and denser and maintains its straightness better.

Card

Mountboard

This is a relatively soft, fine display board obtainable from art and graphics shops or picture framers. An A1 sheet will average £3. It is a good constructional material for medium-size forms and the black version is useful for model boxes. Although there are cheaper versions available, the type commonly stocked is the Studland brand from Daler-Rowney. This comes in a standard A1 (594 × 841mm) size, is 1.4mm thick (or 1,400microns as it's usually measured) and consists of one side covered with a coloured paper, while the other side is left white. The choice of colours tends towards pastel because the card is designed to be cut into frames, or passepartouts,when mounting drawings or prints under glass. The coloured surface is also usually matt and very sensitive to marking. Thinner mountboard, for example 1,000 microns, is also available, but usually only from specialized paper shops.

The Daler version is easy to cut smoothly, although some cheaper versions tend to be harder. It is not suitable for slender or intricate forms, partly because of its thickness in scale (1.4mm makes 35mm at 1:25 scale, which is not bad for a chair leg but too chunky for a window frame), but also because it is too fragile at that size. It will also tend to separate into layers when you try to cut a strip any thinner than about 3mm wide. It will not bend readily and if curved shapes are needed the card has to be scored in repeated lines to assist it (*see* Chapter 2).

Stencil paper

This is a strong, oiled paper suitable for cutting intricate forms, also known as oiled manila. It can be found in most art shops or specialist paper shops and averages £2.50 for an A1 sheet. Because of its natural, wood-like colour it is a good surfacing material for wood effects. It is more a thin card than a paper (300microns or 0.3mm thick). The linseed oil serves two purposes. Firstly, it stops the paper from absorbing water while stencilling, which lengthens the working life of the stencil. Secondly, it gives the paper a smoother composition, which enables quite intricate cutting and eases the friction on the scalpel blade (similar to cutting through wax). Despite this, the card is surprisingly rigid for its thickness. It is ideal for cutting window frames or for building up moulding profiles where mountboard would be too thick.

Foamboard

Foamboard is a very light, thick, stable board which consists of foamed polystyrene sandwiched between tough paper layers. It is found in any art or graphics shop. An A1 sheet of 5mm foamboard will vary between £4–£6 (it is usually also sold in 3.5mm and 10mm thicknesses). It can be used for building quick and sturdy sketch models and for white-card models in film and architecture. It is also used for building theatre model-boxes or as a mount for soldering templates.

Depending upon where it comes from, it is known variously as foamcore, featherboard or polyboard. White is most often used, but it also comes in black. No colours are produced as yet. It can be glued (surface to surface, or edge to surface) with PVA (preferably the Loctite, Weldbond or Evo-Stick 'fast-grip' variety), so there is usually no need to use a special foam glue. Edge-to-edge gluing will not be very strong, whatever one uses. Avoid UHU as this will dissolve the foam interior on most brands and spray paints will do the same. It should not be confused with Kapa-line foamboard when attempting to use it as a sculptural or textural material. The paper covering cannot be removed easily and the foam itself is very fragile.

Kapa-line foamboard

This is a superior type of foamboard with a polyurethane (rather than polystyrene) foam centre that can be found in art shops and model shops. It is more expensive than standard foamboard, on average £6 for a 30 × 40in (76cm × 102cm) sheet. Apart from being used as a normal foamboard for all of the above, the interior foam can be used for a variety of sculptural or textural effects. Many years ago this seemed to be the type of foamboard most available, but then cheaper brands flooded the market. What is special about Kapa-line, and what sometimes justifies the higher price, is that the paper layer can be carefully peeled off. The foam inside can be carved, sanded and will take impressions particularly well. It will also glue more readily with PVA than the standard polystyrene versions and solvent-based glues such as UHU do not dissolve it.

Materials for mould-making and casting

Mould-making

Silicone rubber

This is the best choice when a flexible mould is needed and fine detail has to be faithfully reproduced. Silicone rubbers are the most widely used professionally. They come in many varieties, with different degrees of hardness, setting times and methods of application. They are fairly expensive (averaging at £25 per litre) and their shelf-life (the amount of time they keep after buying them) may be limited to six to twelve months.

The Shore A number denotes hardness when cured, or set. For example, the type featured in Chapter 3 (RTV-101 from Tiranti) is relatively hard at Shore A 55. Often these harder silicones will also be heat-resistant. (RTV-101 can be heated up to 260°C, for example, which means that it is suitable for making castings in low-melt metals, plus a polymer clay such as Super Sculpey can be press-moulded into it and baked in a domestic oven.) Most silicones can be poured and come in two parts, comprising the rubber itself and a liquid catalyst. These have to be properly mixed for the rubber to cure. Directions are usually clear and straightforward as to how many drops of catalyst are needed per 100g of rubber (the usual by weight is around 5 per cent of catalyst to rubber, but dropper bottles make dosing a lot easier). There is often a comfortable margin for error! A calibrated beaker is necessary for measuring out the rubber and this (together with any mixing sticks used) should be as clean as possible because most substances which harden by chemical reaction are sensitive to contamination. This may result in the silicone not curing properly, or needing a longer time to do it.

Depending upon the type, silicones need anything from a couple of hours to a few days to cure normally. Adding less than the average recommended amount of catalyst may lengthen the working time but also the curing time. Adding more will have the opposite effect. Most pouring silicones can be altered by the addition of a special thickening agent which turns them into a spreadable gel. This means that they can be brushed onto the surface of a prototype as a thick layer (rather than cast as a block), saving on the amount of silicone used. On its own, this thick skin would be too flexible to make casts from, so it needs to be held in place by a separate 'jacket' of plaster cast over the top. The thickening agent will tend to cause the mixture to start setting more quickly, so speed is crucial when using this method.

Although silicones can't be re-melted in the way that vinyl can, one useful economy can be made with moulds no longer needed. They can be chopped into little pieces and used to 'pack' new moulds in the making. As long as the rubber is like-for-like, and as long as the prototype is first coated with some of the fresh mix, the rest of the mould can be largely recycled filling, bound together with more of the fresh mix. It is possible to save considerably on the amount of new rubber one has to use in this way. As long as there are no air gaps, there will be little difference in the mould's elasticity or strength.

On the whole, one needn't worry about trapped air bubbles when using either silicone or polyurethane rubbers. The curing time is so long that any trapped air, being much lighter than the rubber, will work its way to the surface long before the rubber starts to harden.

Polyurethane rubber

Polyurethane rubbers have very similar properties to silicones, but the main difference is that most are supplied and mixed in two equal parts (parts 'A' and 'B'). Some are tougher than silicones and better suited to casting in abrasive materials such as concrete. Like silicones, they also come in a range of hardnesses and other properties. Whereas silicones are unaffected by a wide range of prototyping and casting materials, and often no special barrier or release agent is required (although a thin coat of vaseline always helps), the same is *not* true for polyurethanes. You must fully acquaint yourself with the technical data and recommendations supplied with the product. Often special sealing or release agents are recommended and this should be taken seriously, otherwise you may end up with a mould that's completely stuck to the prototype, or a mould full of rubber that refuses to set (because the polyurethane has reacted to something on the prototype which inhibits the curing process). Certainly, you can't use polyurethane rubber to make a mould and then cast polyurethane resin into that mould without the proper release agent – they will stick inseparably to each other without it. That's why, on the whole, it's better to use silicone rubbers as much as possible just in case you decide later to try castings in polyurethane resin.

Gelflex

This is the brand name for one type of re-meltable vinyl, another being Vinamold. Both are available in either 'hard' or 'soft', although even the hard versions are relatively soft compared to some silicones. Gelflex is supplied in blocks and needs to be melted at around 140°C before it will become liquid enough to pour over a prototype. This means that only heat-resistant prototypes are suitable, but polymer clay, wood or plaster will serve the purpose. When it has set, Gelflex forms a flexible mould similar to rubber, but not nearly as durable. There is a limit to the number of 'pulls' (castings) that can be made from a vinyl mould before the surface deteriorates or the mould itself starts to tear. In addition, Gelflex is unsuitable for reproducing fine detail because it starts thickening immediately on contact with the cold prototype and deeper detail may therefore be lost.

The main advantages of using this type of vinyl are speed and cost. The mould is ready to be used as soon as it is cool, which could be under an hour for a small form (a larger block of Gelflex may need a good few hours to cool and set; it's best to wait as long as possible because even though the surface might feel firm and cooled, the centre could still be soft). The main advantage is that it is much cheaper than silicone by weight (averaging £5 a kilo), but old moulds can also be re-melted more than a few times. This makes it the best choice for making simple castings on a low budget.

Although expensive heating units are available, Gelflex can be melted in an ordinary saucepan on a low heat (a milk saucepan with a pouring lip is useful). If this is done, however, precautions are very important! Ventilation must be good because fumes are given off in the process and the melting Gelflex must be constantly watched and stirred. It will turn a greenish colour if it overheats. This will produce more fumes and will also shorten the life of the Gelflex for future use.

Gelflex will accept both polyurethane resin and plaster without the need for a release agent. Another useful advantage of Gelflex is that, because of its low melting point, the inside surface of the mould can be smoothed using a heat gun. This can sometimes do a better job of removing surface imperfections than sanding the prototype, although this technique requires a lot of practice and experiment to get the level of heat, distance and duration right.

Latex

Liquid latex sets by evaporation of the water within it, so it is ready to be used without any mixing of parts. However, because of this evaporation it shrinks noticeably as it dries –anything up to 10 per cent. This, and the fact that it can only be built up in layers, make it unsuitable for any serious or detailed mould-making. A 'sock' or 'glove' mould could be made by building up layers on a very simple shape (preferably of plaster), peeling it off when dry and casting plaster into it. This might need anything from four to ten separate coats to make a mould with any strength. A thicker collar of latex should be included at the base of the mould to stop it from collapsing and to hang it from when pouring the plaster. There will inevitably be some distortion of the form.

Plaster

Plaster is more often used in model-making as a casting than a mould-making material because of its inflexibility. One exception might be when a slightly flexible material such as Super Sculpey is press-moulded into a plaster mould, as described in Chapter 3. Another occasional exception might be the technique known as 'waste moulding', which is suitable for making just one copy of a form where undercutting is not a particular issue. The form to be copied is first covered with a thick shell of one of the softer plasters, usually in a few layers. As long as the prototype can be extracted from the plaster shell there may be no need to make this in two parts. A hollow plaster receptacle remains, and if one then fills this with a much harder plaster the softer plaster can be carefully chipped away from it once set, hence the 'waste' part. The mould is also destroyed in the process. A good barrier such as mould-maker's soap or vaseline is needed on the inside of the mould.

It is common for the shell to be built up with a relatively thin layer of plaster first to get into the details (often by a technique of 'flicking' wet plaster onto the surface with the hand). This is then followed by a layer of plaster-soaked fabric such as jute scrim. This serves to strengthen the shell, but it doesn't need to be particularly thick (performing the same function as glass-fibre matting in resin lamination). This also helps when chipping the shell away at the end because it will detach itself in larger pieces.

Casting

Polyurethane resin

Like its rubber counterpart, polyurethane resin comes in two equal parts for easier mixing. It is available in both clear and opaque versions and special colourings can also be added to the mix. The type featured in Chapter 3 (DRO 29 from Tiranti) starts as two clear liquids which become an opaque ivory when set. This happens rapidly, the pot life (the amount of time it stays pourable after mixing) being only a matter of minutes. Cast elements can be removed from the mould in as little as fifteen minutes. They will not yet be set totally hard, but will be hard enough to detach from the mould; full setting may take a few days. This 'green' (still soft and flexible) stage is useful for trimming the forms. A resin of this type is essential for any casting of detailed or slender forms. Even a fine, hard casting plaster would be too fragile. Polyurethane resin accepts acrylic or enamel paint well, though a much better painting surface is obtained by spraying with Simoniz car primer first.

Polyester resin

This is the material normally used in conjunction with glass-fibre matting to produce fibreglass. What results is a very hard shell, which, depending upon the number of applied layers, is extremely rigid and weight-supporting. The most common use in the 'real' world is for boat-building, where a durable but light shell is needed for the hull. In theatre and film, it serves to reinforce landscaped areas, making them fit to walk on. But there is usually little justification for going to this trouble in a model of average size, where load-bearing strength is usually not an issue and where there are other, simpler ways of constructing a shell with adequate strength.

Polyester resin is also normally used for clear castings, that is, as a means of embedding an object in clear plastic. For this purpose special clear-casting resins have been developed, as opposed to the more general-purpose type for fibreglass lamination. As a material, it is so fraught with complication that there is, again, little point in using it unless it's definitely the only option! The only other advantage to it is that many polyesters have a relatively lengthy curing time, which means that they have a long pot life and so can be used (with the addition of fillers and pigments to create opacity) as a tough gap-filling lacquer to build up a smooth shell on a form. Most other resins would start to set too quickly for this.

Polyester resin hardens with the addition of a catalyst and here the most exact measurements are crucial, because if too much catalyst is added the chemical reaction produces a lot of heat, which can cause the whole thing to crack. There may be this danger anyway because the chemical reaction produces more heat the more plastic is mixed, so a large block could harbour awesome temperatures at its core. The percentage of catalyst recommended is small, so there is less room for error. Many other factors can affect the curing, such as temperature and humidity, but especially the mould material, or, in the case of clear casting, whatever you're pouring it on top of. It is best to read the manufacturer's recommendations for treatment of these surfaces prior to using it.

Plaster

Most of the plasters found in DIY centres for small building jobs are usually too coarse, soft or slow-setting to serve any purpose here. The plaster labelled as 'plaster of Paris' is not necessarily a special type (the phrase just means 'plaster' or gypsum and originates from the fact that there was a large gypsum deposit outside Paris). If you find this either in a DIY centre, chemist or hobby shop, there is no guarantee that it will be fine or strong enough for small castings and it should be tested first. The surest choice is a proper casting plaster such as Basic Alpha or

Crystacal, from a sculptor's suppliers such as Tiranti. Basic Alpha (featured in Chapter 3) is very fine, quick-setting and hard. Directions for mixing it (the plaster is always added to the water) are given in the chapter. Some sculptors prefer to mix it exactly according to the optimum plaster/water ratio. In the case of Basic Alpha this is 2.8k/ltr. There are even harder plasters, usually requiring a higher proportion of plaster to water.

Basic Alpha can be made even stronger by mixing it with a special plaster polymer (an acrylic resin) in place of water. Plaster and resin need to be mixed faithfully (three parts plaster to one part polymer), rather than the usual 'by eye' method. For large amounts power-assisted mixing is recommended, but small amounts can easily be mixed by hand as long as this is vigorous. What results is a creamy mixture that will set exceptionally hard and is much less brittle than the water-mixed plaster. It can even be used, with appropriate matting, as an alternative to laminating resin without the harmful vapours. It is a little too thick to flow in the way that the polyurethane resin will, but is perfect for larger forms, also working out cheaper at about £6 per litre.

Polymer clay

The technique of casting using a clay substance is not very common because it is unlikely that any normal clay will set in a mould and in any case there's the question of how to get the clay in there in the first place. Clay is, of course, commonly used for casting pottery, but in its liquid form, slip. The emergence of polymer clays that can be fired hard at relatively low temperatures, combined with the development of silicone rubbers that can withstand these same oven temperatures, have really opened up the possibilities of using this method.

The easiest technique is to press-mould Super Sculpey into a flat one-piece mould as demonstrated in Chapter 3. The resultant 'pull' can either be laid unaltered on a ceramic tile or baking tray in the oven, or the shape can be modified (the Sculpey leaf shapes, for example). This method makes it possible to create a large number of casts, or variations, in a short time.

But Sculpey can also be cast in a two-piece mould with a bit of extra care. This involves pressing softened Sculpey into the two halves of the mould separately, just proud of the dividing edges. The two mould halves are then pressed together (in a kind of turning/rocking motion to join the clay together – this needs to be practised!). The excess clay should be squeezed out along the seam line and should be trimmed off when baked. The whole set-up goes in the oven, for a little longer than the time recommended on the polymer clay packet. Of course, this is only possible with the appropriate mould rubber, such as RTV-101.

Latex

In the context of casting materials, latex has just one use, but a significant one. The practice of making latex skin, or surface, casts is quite common in model-making and was used extensively in film until silicone started replacing latex. It involves making a flat 3-D negative of a surface feature or pronounced texture, onto which latex is then painted in a number of layers. When completely dry, the latex can be peeled away, having formed a positive copy. This skin can then be glued onto a flat surface or wrapped and stretched around one that's not flat. One can therefore generate an unlimited supply of a particular surface effect for a wide variety of applications.

It's not worth trying to brush latex into a mould, as the brush will become unusable very quickly, however careful you are about rinsing it between applications. A better and quicker method is to pour more latex than you need directly into the mould, rock it around until the whole surface is covered, then pour the excess back into the pot. If you stop once the dripping finishes you'll know that there's neither too much nor too little latex for the layer. It can take anything from thirty minutes to an hour to dry, depending upon the material of the mould. If it is plaster, the process is quite speedy because the plaster will absorb water from the latex mixture, but if it is sealed styrofoam or plastic the drying time will be quite a bit longer.

Special latex colours are available to add to the mix if you want a base colouring to the skin. This is always a good idea because you can judge the resultant texture much better. Only a very minimal amount of colouring is needed because the latex itself is semi-transparent. Most concentrated toners for emulsion paint (available from decorating stores) will work just as well.

Successful painting of latex is more of a problem, however. Straight acrylic might adhere to the surface at first, but will crack and peel off in time because it is not being allowed to key properly. There are other methods, such as mixing some acrylic with latex to form a paint, but this is not guaranteed to work. What does adhere to latex very well is enamel paint. It will tend to react with the latex surface, however, and so its drying time will be longer than usual, although it will not be unreasonable. The enamel paint will also stretch with the latex to an extent without flaking.

Modelling materials

Super Sculpey

The particular type featured in this book is Super Sculpey,

which is flesh-coloured and available in 1lb boxes. The price averages £7 a box, making it more economical than others in the Sculpey range. It is a polymer 'clay', in fact largely a type of plastic, and needs to be heated up before it will harden (FIMO is another similar material). Although the manufacturers recommend baking it in a domestic oven (130°C is sufficient), it can be hardened just as easily and more quickly under a heat gun on medium setting (full details on working with it are included in Chapter 5).

The supreme virtue of Sculpey is that it possesses even more softness and 'plasticity' (when worked a little between the fingers) than plasticine without any of the stickiness. Some synthetic modelling materials have a certain tough elasticity, meaning that when one tries to make a slight impression they will resist a bit, which makes modelling with them frustrating. This doesn't happen with Super Sculpey. Its other virtue is that an unfinished form can be hardened, either totally or partially, to form a more stable base for further modelling. Fresh Sculpey will stick to hardened material without any problem and there is seemingly no limit to the number of times the same piece can be subjected to heat as long as the level of heat remains under that recommended.

Milliput

This is an epoxy putty which consists of two parts that have to be mixed together thoroughly in equal amounts. When mixed, it has roughly the same consistency as plasticine or Sculpey, but will begin to harden (depending upon room temperature) after about forty minutes. Within just a few hours it will become rock hard, but this can be accelerated to minutes if heated. It is partially soluble in water until it hardens, so water can be used to soften and smooth the surface. However, because of this it also softens with moisture from the fingers and so the fingertips do tend to get 'gunged up' quite quickly, which can make detailed modelling difficult. It will also stick too much to modelling tools. There are five different types available, white being the finest and more expensive at around £6 for a 4oz pack. Standard Milliput is yellow-grey, coarser and cheaper. Black and terracotta are the other colours available. When Milliput is more thoroughly 'cut' with water it can be used as a gap-filling adhesive, a soft filler, or even as a relief paint.

Plasticine

The most available type of plasticine is Newplast, made by Lewis, in 500g packets (averaging £1) with a range of colours. Most people will be familiar with this material and guess that it is only suitable for temporary work because it never hardens. It is very malleable, but too soft for professional modelling. It tends to melt on the fingers, making fine work difficult. Putting work in the fridge for a while will help a little, but only temporarily. A little more durability can be given to plasticine by coating it (perhaps two to three times) with PVA. This will give it a slightly tougher skin which can then be painted. Forms created this way will last but they still have to be handled with care, because the soft plasticine is merely contained within a thin flexible skin. It can be used as a filler in emergencies if sufficiently coated in this way. It is more useful for modelling prototypes from which moulds can be made, especially in plaster because it is water-repellent.

Chavant clays

These professional oil-based clays have a similar composition to plasticine, but are available in three degrees of hardness and two standard colours (grey-green and terracotta). Apart from being easier to work with, they are non-sulphurated, meaning that they are more compatible with silicone rubber when making moulds. Chavant clays are industry standard, along with Sculpey, for the creation of character maquettes, but the harder variety is also suitable for modelling precise streamline forms such as car models because it can be worked to an immaculate finish.

'Green stuff'

This is an affectionate name, widely used, for a product similar to Milliput. Its actual name is Kneadatite. Like Milliput, it comes in two equal parts which have to be kneaded together (in this case, a strong yellow and blue component, from whence arrives the 'green' of its stage name). Its advantages over Milliput include that it accepts even finer detail and has a longer working life before it starts hardening (one and a half to two and a half hours according to room temperature – the lower the temperature, the longer the time). Full hardening will take about twenty-four hours.

Like Milliput, it's partially soluble in water, a property that can be used for smoothing or cleaning. It is supplied with the yellow and blue strips already stuck to each other. This may assist in measuring out equal amounts, but it also means that where these touch the material will have begun to harden. The manufacturers recommend cutting this middle strip away, so already there has been a bit of wastage! This may not matter except for the fact that Kneadatite is expensive compared to the alternatives. When mixed, it is extremely sticky (even on metal), which is an advantage when working with armatures but causes problems when trying to model. Even fans of the material have likened it to trying to sculpt with bubblegum! Lastly, although it accepts paint well, green is hardly a natural colour to want to model with.

Air-drying clays

These have long been considered something only for children, because originally this type of clay was a form of pulped paper and as such had a coarse, uneven consistency. The material was also prone to heavy shrinkage and cracking. Now there are many different types available. Many are still fibrous and so not suitable for fine detail, and anything which dries by evaporation will inevitably shrink. But they are cheap, on the whole, and can be used as a basis form as long as they're given enough time to dry thoroughly.

Materials for creating surfaces

Texturing materials

Polyfilla

Originally a specific brand name, the word has now become a blanket term to describe a wide variety of water-based fillers for repairing wall surfaces and other home decorating jobs. These fillers dry by evaporation and are invariably white. Although some still come in powder form, most are now sold ready-mixed. Properties vary quite significantly according to the brand, including how well they stick to surfaces, how much they shrink and how hard they dry. On the whole, the most effective ones for model-making purposes are the so-called 'fine surface' fillers because these can be spread more thinly and will achieve more detail. The particular brand recommended here is the fine surface version made by the original Polyfilla firm, Polycell. This is more akin to an acrylic paste and will stick to almost anything, however thinly applied. Shrinkage is minimal and it dries tough but also remains quite flexible. This makes it ideal for giving a slightly more durable surface to styrofoam, for example, where other plastic fillers would dissolve the surface. For more about texturing with it see Chapter 6. If mixed with water to an even, creamy consistency it can be used as a relief paint and this is described in Chapter 5. Alternatively, inert substances such as sand, granulated cork, ground olive stones or fine gravel can be added to create even more textural possibilities.

Similar products worth noting here are Idenden Brushcoat or Rosco Foamcoat, both made specifically for scenic texturing and widely used in theatre and film. They are even stickier and

more flexible when dry. They could be useful to the model-maker if they were available in smaller amounts, the smallest for Idenden being 10kg, for example. On the other side of the scale, there are whole systems of texturing or impasto pastes, some with gritty additives, to supplement acrylic paints and available from art shops. These tend to be overpriced for the amount one gets and the polyfilla cited above will generally do just as good a job at a fraction of the cost.

Two-part fillers

These usually consist of either an epoxy or polyester resin with some inert filling substance already mixed in and come either in two equal parts or a bulk part and a catalyst. These need to be thoroughly mixed together for the filler to harden. The main advantage over water-based fillers is that they set by chemical reaction rather than evaporation so they will not shrink. They can therefore fill much bigger gaps or be applied more thickly. For model-making purposes another advantage is that they are unlikely to warp the surface they're applied to. But they are expensive and their fumes can pose a health hazard. Car body fillers of this type can usually be found where car maintenance products are sold.

Cladding Materials

Obeche wood

This is a very popular wood with model-makers, being relatively soft, pliable and easy to cut while being harder and more resilient than balsa. It comes in sheets down to 0.8mm thick, as well as a range of rods and strips. Although common in model shops it is rare to find it anywhere else. It is light in colour, of a medium density and accepts stain very well. The grain is not obtrusive, although certain structures appear when staining so tests need to be made first.

Balsa wood

This is perhaps one of the most familiar model-making materials for 'early years' and certainly a cheap one, but is not so widely used professionally because it is so fragile. It can be useful as a surfacing material though, especially where the effect of rough, weathered beams is needed, because balsa can be easily broken down with a wire-brush along the grain. It will take paint and glue well, but staining often appears washed out with a silvery sheen. It can usually be found in blocks, strips or sheets down to about 1mm.

Walnut, bass and spruce

These are the other woods most commonly available in model shops. Walnut has a darker colour and is more brittle and harder to cut than obeche. Bass is very light in colour and relatively soft, without much of a noticeable grain. This can be a better choice for cutting intricate or curved shapes. Spruce has a very prominent grain emphasized by resinous lines. This may be good sometimes for floorboards but it also makes spruce harder to cut evenly with the scalpel.

Cork sheet

This can make an interesting surface texture and is surprisingly durable. It will accept paint well and can be mounted either with Spray Mount, PVA or contact adhesive. There is a range of grades and thicknesses, the thinnest being about a millimetre. Thicker sheets can be broken down a little using a wire brush or knife point.

Kapa-line foamboard

Unlike the standard, cheaper foamboard, the surfacing paper on Kapa can be peeled away. What remains is an even sheet of very impressionable polyurethane foam which can be scored, carved, sanded or imprinted. The foam is not 'springy', staying put when pressed, and will not expand when painted. It will accept even thin washes of paint very well and its ivory colour makes a good base. Polyurethane is resistant to most solvents, so, unlike styrofoam, it can be sprayed with even acetone-based paints and will accept most glues. It is available in thicknesses of 3mm, 5mm or 10mm.

Styrofoam

Although mainly useful as a building material, and more commonly available in thick sheets or blocks, thinner sheets (down to 1mm) can be found in more specialist model shops. These can be scored or embossed in much the same way as Kapa, though not quite as well because of a slight skin on the surface. Styrofoam will dissolve in solvents such as acetone, which limits the choice of glues and paints. Its fine-celled structure is very easy to cut, carve or sand to a smooth finish. Different densities are available.

Foamed PVC

For more about this material, see 'Materials for Construction' or Chapter 2. In itself, foamed PVC sheet has no interesting surface texture, but being relatively soft it can be scraped with coarse sandpaper to give it a fake grain which can suggest wood reasonably well when painted. Lines can also be easily embossed using a hard point.

Latex

The technique of using liquid latex to create textural skins is described in Chapter 3. Latex is available from sculpture suppliers and some art or hobby shops. It averages at around £8 per litre. Moulds for casting the skins can be made from either Kapa-line foam or plaster. Although the former are quicker to make, latex will dry more rapidly on plaster and detach itself more easily. Two coats are usually needed to form a strong layer, the first left to dry properly before the second is added.

Vinyl wallpapers

These are composed of a soft paper layer onto which a foamed plastic pattern is printed. There are countless organic, floral or geometric patterns to choose from and DIY centres will often have opened rolls on the shelves from which to take samples. They will take paint well, though the vinyl pattern will tend to resist a very thin wash. This can, however, be used to good effect to accentuate the pattern.

Decorative papers

A visit to a specialist paper shop such as Paperchase will present many other options for using ready-made surfaces. Patterned writing paper may provide just the right marble effect, or there are other, larger sheets with a variety of embossed patterns. Many hobby shops now have a whole section devoted to card and scrapbook decoration and this has also become a good source of unusual paper surfaces.

Sandpaper

Abrasive papers come in a variety of grades and can offer a cleaner, quicker alternative for creating surfaces such as asphalt or pebbledash. It is sometimes difficult to imagine how the surface will read when painted, so it is a good idea to build up a collection of painted samples. Also, the effect produced can be too uniform to be realistic and may need to be enhanced by gluing extra sand in places.

Oil-painting paper

This is supplied as an alternative to canvas and has a fine canvas imprint. It has already been treated with a layer of primer suitable for oil- or spirit-based paints, but will accept other paints if they are not too thin. The slight texture can give a flat colour a little more vibrancy even if no obvious texture is needed in the model. It is worth considering spray-mounting it onto PVC or card for a more versatile painting surface. It can also suggest worn, woven carpet especially as thin paints can be rubbed away, exposing the texture more.

Stencil paper

As evidenced in Chapter 6, stencil paper has a sympathetic wood-like surface which can be further enhanced by staining. Although the paper has been impregnated with linseed oil to make it tougher, it will accept water-based paints and PVA to some extent. It is available from most art or graphics suppliers.

Velour

The term 'velour' is often used to denote the adhesive plastic material found in hobby or decorating centres, or various types of flocked paper. These are useful for representing black masking curtains in a theatre set model, small-scale grass or carpets. An appropriately thin paint or ink needs to be used if the surface requires painting.

Scatter Materials

Granulated cork

This is sold specifically in model shops for creating scenic effects and usually comes in three different grades: coarse, medium and fine. It is cheap, light and takes glue and paint very well. It can even be dyed, although its natural brown colour limits the range. It is ideal for changing the consistency of polyfilla without adding to the weight, for example in achieving convincing earth effects.

Sand and grit

Sand is an obvious choice for fixing with glue to create a texture or adding to a polyfilla mix, but may not be so easy to get hold of in small amounts. The best option is to collect a little as and when you next see it. Model shops may stock a variety of scenic sands and grits down to a very fine grade, otherwise pet shops are a good source for sand, as well as for different types of gravel or fine stones for aquariums. If rather pushed in terms of time, the kitchen can offer some solutions – sugar can be used instead of sand or instant coffee instead of grit, for example. Both can be sprinkled into PVA without loosing too much of their structure. They need to be properly sealed, however, preferably with a spirit-based paint, otherwise they are unlikely to last.

Vermiculite

This is a naturally occurring mineral which expands when heated. It is sold in granulated form as an insulation material in building and can also be found in garden centres as a soil filler. It is popular with scenic workshops for creating a heavily textured paint because it is light and inert, that is, it will not affect the properties of the paint. As it comes, it can make convincing stones for scenic models, but can easily be broken down further for other effects.

Sawdust

One advantage of sawdust is that it can be dyed, stained or glued so well. Model shops usually sell a range of greens and browns for scenic effects, otherwise different grades of sawdust can be found in pet shops.

Poppy seeds

Found in the supermarket (usually in the baking section), poppy seeds are quite effective for representing pebbles at a small scale. Also, because they are quite regular in size and shape, they suggest small leaves such as privet very well, as illustrated at the end of Chapter 6.

Sisal

Chapter 6 describes a method for creating a grass effect using clumps of dyed sisal pulled from the special mats for lining hanging flower baskets. Garden centres are therefore the best source for this material. Sisal is a natural fibre used in rope-making and carpeting.

Eggshell

Most scatter materials are granular, but at times a material more like flakes or plates might be needed to create a certain effect. A case in point is provided by the technique for suggesting leaves in Chapter 4. Eggshells can be easily crushed to form leaf-like particles; if a proper mortar and pestle is used the size can be controlled.

Tea

The tea powder from used teabags makes a very good soil, either scattered into glue or mixed into a paste with PVA or paint.

Painting, staining, dyeing and finishing materials

Painting

Primer

Primer is a special, cheaper paint for sealing absorbent surfaces prior to painting. It may not be necessary in all cases, but is advisable. It also helps to prevent warping if a non-water-based primer is used. Primer will provide a better key for painting on plastics or metals and is available either in brushable or spray form.

Acrylic paint

Acrylic is a water-based paint, most familiar from art suppliers in tube form, although nowadays many household paints also have an acrylic base. A better range of colour is achievable with acrylic than perhaps with any other paint except oil. It is one of the most versatile forms of paint. However, it is designed for comparatively rapid use and hardly has one mixed up a colour on the palette before it starts to dry out! Tube acrylic needs quite a bit of encouragement before it thins properly with water and the results are often unsatisfactory. If used straight from the tube it clogs detail, deposits visible brush strokes and leaves an undesirable silky finish which is neither one thing nor the other … and usually totally unsuitable

considering most natural or natural-looking surfaces tend to be matt!

An exception might be the more liquid acrylic mixes designed for airbrush work and available in plastic bottles (for example, DecoArt's Americana or the range from Inscribe). These will not dry so quickly, coverage is better and thinner, and they generally dry more matt.

Gouache

Gouache is quite simply watercolour paint which has been made more opaque with the addition of fillers. It can be very versatile, can be thinned down more easily and is relatively inexpensive. If it dries, it can be dissolved again with water, but this makes it unsuitable for overpainting, or building up 'glazes' of paint because a second application will immediately mix with the one underneath it. If used as it comes, it needs to be spray-fixed or brushed with a spirit-based sealant or varnish if you want to preserve it, especially on objects which are going to be handled such as model figures. A better alternative would be to mix an equal amount of PVA glue with it to make it self-sealing. This will also help it to adhere to non-porous surfaces such as plastic.

Enamel paint

This is a fast-drying, oil-based paint available in small tins that has been developed specifically for painting on plastic. It will therefore usually adhere to anything, covers exceptionally well without streaking, dries matt (if matt versions are chosen) and will keep in the tin for a long time. Being oil- rather than water-based it will not warp any surface, even thin paper, but unlike standard artists' oil paint it will harden properly on paper or card. Satin and gloss versions are also available, with most being very opaque. The main producers are Humbrol or Revell.

One drawback is that the choice of colours tends to concentrate on the muted rather than rich primaries, specific to military model kits. Another is the vapour produced by the solvents. Good ventilation is essential when using them, especially because white spirit needs to be used to thin them or clean brushes. Tins cost around £1.20 in the shops (although they can be cheaper on the Internet) and they can be found in all good model shops and some artists' or hobby shops.

Colourings or 'toners'

These are concentrated paints intended for changing the colour of other paints or materials, for example wall emulsion paint. They are usually available from more specialist decorators' shops. Some colourings are designed to mix with a variety of media including casting resin or latex. They are particularly useful for making a coloured basecoat from standard white emulsion, or changing the colour of polyfilla.

Aerosol paint

Many of the spray paints one sees (for example, the Simoniz brand car body primers available in matt white, mid-grey or brick red, the glossy car colours in garages, or the household spray colours in DIY shops) are cellulose-based and the solvent in them is acetone. This is why they will dissolve the surface of styrofoam and some other plastics; it is also why acetone will clean or dissolve them. They're not very economical to use for overall coverage (for example, to turn a white model box black!) and will release headache-inducing vapours into the air when used in this way. But they're perfect to have on hand (even if it's just matt black, grey or rust) for slightly modifying painted surfaces, such as to tone down, to darken and so on. If surfaces to be sprayed are sprinkled liberally with sand or sugar before spraying a very satisfying mottled or fragmented effect can be achieved, especially if repeated with more than one colour. Otherwise using a spray paint has advantages if you want to achieve a very flat, even surface without brush marks.

French enamel varnish

Usually referred to as FEV for short, this comes in a number of transparent colours. It has natural shellac as a base. FEV is fairly fast drying and can be used as a coloured glaze on glass and plastic. It is also useful for staining and varnishing wood at the same time.

Staining and dyeing

Wood stain

There are many available, either water-based or spirit-based, their colours corresponding to the types of wood intended. Spirit-based stains tend to infiltrate better and will not warp the base material. They are expensive, though, if it is necessary to experiment with different colours; mixture of white spirit and pigment (from pastels, shoe polish and so on) generally works just as well.

Liquid shoe polish

These work quite well on wood or cardboard to create a polished wood colour, getting progressively richer and shinier with each coat. They are usually water-based, which may lead to warping.

Inks

Apart from a range of bottled inks available from art materials shops, the leftover ink from inkjet cartridges makes strong and vibrant colours. This can be thinned with water, but it needs to be sealed or a little binder such as PVA can be added. The results are not fade-proof, however.

Dylon dye

This dye powder can also be mixed with white spirit or with hot water to make quite a powerful stain. Otherwise it can be used as intended for dyeing materials in a hot bath (such as a saucepan on the stove) with the addition of salt. Scatter materials such as granulated cork or sawdust can be customized in this way. Rice or shredded coconut can be given very strong colours, even rich black, to provide other interesting alternatives.

Finishing

PVA

If only a sealant is required to protect a fragile or powdery surface, heavily diluted PVA may be sufficient. There will be a slight change on a matt paint surface. Increasing the amount of PVA will make a good satin varnish and successive coats will increase the shine.

Polish

Often spraying a painted surface with a little furniture polish, leaving for a while and then buffing with a rag, will produce a satisfying result. The advantage here over liquid varnishes is that the inside corners remain a little matt rather than glossy, which improves the overall effect. Straight varnish will tend to look too glossy and will highlight every imperfection.

Special effects

Glass frosting

Available only as a spray, glass frosting will produce a translucent frosted effect on glass or acetate. A quick, light spray will produce a light frosting that can be intensified with further coats.

Metalcote

Made by Humbrol, this type of enamel needs preferably to be painted on a hard smooth surface. The paint must be left to dry thoroughly, then it can be buffed with a rag to produce a convincing metallic finish. It is available for various metal effects ranging from aluminium to gunmetal.

Finger Gold

A suspension of metallic particles in a waxy base, which, as the name implies, can be rubbed on with the finger. When buffed with a rag the particles settle flat and produce a very reflective surface. This will work better on a smooth, dark ground.

Adhesives and solvents

Adhesives

Adhesives differ mainly according to, first of all, the ease with which they find all those microscopic purchase points on surfaces (rather like a rock climber), in other words, how fluid they start or how 'sticky' they are. Then it depends upon the means by which they harden, that is, by evaporation of a solvent within or by a chemical reaction. Finally, they differ according to how hard and inflexible they can become.

PVA

PVA is one of the best glues for general purposes, effective on most porous surfaces such as card and wood. The initials stand for 'polyvinyl acetate'. PVA allows for some repositioning, but relies on surfaces being tightly pressed together to bond. As it dries it contracts, pulling the joint together even tighter. Even when fully dry it will still be slightly flexible and shock-resistant, which is why it's used commonly in carpentry. It is water-based and dries by evaporation, so will not be effective if air can't get

to it somehow. It also relies on establishing a purchase on a microstructure and being at least partially absorbed, which is why it will not work on plastic or metal (foam is an exception because of its porous nature). Weak gluing between plastic or metal can be achieved sometimes by roughening the surfaces and creating purchase points.

It's important for the model-maker to distinguish between a concentrated PVA such as wood glue (Evo-Stik Wood Adhesive is a popular make) and the weaker, diluted 'school glue' types. Proper wood glue will usually be much more effective and versatile. PVA also serves as a good binder for pigment, as a useful varnish or sealant and, when heavily diluted, as an effective fixative. Standard PVA is not strictly waterproof, although waterproof versions are available. Another special form of PVA worth mentioning here is 'Hi-Tack', which is ideal for scattering materials into because it is stickier and slow-drying.

Superglue

A rapid setting glue, which is more effective the less one doses. Superglue (cyanoacrylate) doesn't harden by evaporation but by reacting with traces of water (specifically ions) to be found on any surface. This is why superglue seems so effective at gluing fingers together while the thing to be glued remains at times blissfully unaffected. This is also why it works so fast. Unlike PVA, it is brittle when hard, so if too much is used between a joint there is the danger that the superglue itself will shatter if jolted. It will achieve a weak bond on metal, mainly for this reason, but this can again be assisted by roughening the surfaces. Accelerators are available in bottle or spray form which will harden the glue even faster on contact. It is better to dose the former using a needle and syringe, while the latter can be both wasteful and harmful because most ends up in the air. Neither superglue nor accelerator is pleasant to have in one's working atmosphere. If mistakes are made (or fingers welded) 'debonders' can be bought which will loosen the glue, but pure acetone will also work.

UHU

UHU was marketed for a long time as a general-purpose glue, although now there are an increasing number of specialized formulations. The 'classic' UHU (in the yellow tube) is transparent and viscous. It is very much a 'convenience glue', effective in emergencies but not really suitable for precise and clean gluing of delicate elements. It can be better than PVA (and an alternative to superglue) for bonding some plastics and light metals. Standard UHU will dissolve styrofoam (and ordinary foamboard foam), but UHU Por has now been developed especially for these.

Contact adhesive

This type of glue is designed for bonding large surfaces, but can also be useful between elements that are difficult to press and hold together. The glue is applied to both surfaces and left to dry until no longer tacky. When the two parts are then pressed together the bond will be immediate with no need for sustained pressure. Contact adhesives generally contain rubber and they remain fairly flexible when dry.

The solvent within them (usually toluene) evaporates and this is both highly flammable and harmful if inhaled. Good ventilation (and preferably a respirator) is essential when gluing large areas. Established makes include Evo-Stik Impact or Dunlop Thixofix.

Epoxy glues

A typical two-part epoxy glue such as Araldite may be the only alternative to soldering for bonding metal. Equal amounts need to be mixed first and different types will vary in their working/setting times. Once set, the bond is very strong.

Plastic solvent

Plastic solvent is a thin, clear liquid that can be used to 'weld' styrene. It is most effective when applied onto the joint and drawn into it. It makes a very clean bond with no visible residue. It can be found in most model shops or obtained from plastics suppliers.

Double-sided tape

This can be useful for gluing large surfaces to each other, especially if you want to avoid warping. It can often be used sparingly, for example placing small strips in key positions. It can also be used for provisional assembly of a construction. A good brand such as 3M will stick well, but cheaper brands vary. If more holding power is needed, carpet tape is a much stronger form.

Spray Mount

This comes in aerosol cans and usually two versions are available: a low-tack spray, which will allow repositioning, and a stronger, more permanent one. Spray Mount is invaluable for gluing large areas of paper or thin card. Other glues will either start drying before the area is coated or will warp the paper. One drawback is that a lot is dispersed around the work area and into the air. Another is that most brands are quite expensive.

Copydex

Copydex is a thin latex glue suitable for bonding fabrics and other extra-porous materials such as cushion foam.

Solvents

Water

Water becomes more effective as a solvent if soap is added, allowing it to penetrate further. For any cleaning purposes in particular this should be tried first before resorting to more harmful substances.

White spirit

Sometimes referred to as 'mineral spirit', white spirit is thin, colourless and derived from petroleum. It can be used in place of the more traditional turpentine for thinning oil-based paints and will not affect their drying time. It is flammable and can cause irritation to the skin. It is a good basis for making stains (for example, by dissolving oil pastel or polish in it), or for turning ordinary pencils into aquarelle pencils (*see* Chapter 7).

Turpentine

This is more expensive than white spirit and is favoured by oil painters. If used to thin enamel paint it will affect the drying time. It is flammable and can cause irritation to the skin.

Acetone

This is the only solvent that will remove cellulose paint (for example, car primer, body spray). Special cellulose thinners are available, composed mainly of acetone. Nail varnish removers contain acetone, but most now have protective ingredients that inhibit its action. Pure acetone is available from chemists or some paint centres. It will dissolve polystyrene, styrofoam (some other forms of styrene) superglue, fibreglass resins and biro ink. Highly flammable!

Methylated spirits

Also known as 'denatured alcohol', it has been rendered unfit to drink, hence the mauve colour, which is purely a safety warning. It will dissolve organic resins such as shellac, as well as rubber glue, biro and felt markers. It is very useful for smoothing the surface of polymer clays such as Super Sculpey. Highly flammable!

Lighter fluid

A petroleum spirit, useful for removing some glues such as the residue left by tape. It is also, of course, highly flammable.

Tools

The following list represents the absolutely basic tools. Other tools can always be added, according to personal preference and the special requirements of a job.

Scalpel

This is a precise surgical knife with disposable blades, obtainable from most art suppliers. The standard is from Swann-Morton and the best blades to use are 10A.

Usually two sizes of handle are available, but the smaller is generally easier to use. The advantage of this type of knife over other types (such as X-acto) is that the blade is more supported along its length. Blunted blades can be easily resharpened by stroking both sides on a piece of wet & dry paper (P600 grade or more).

Mechanical pencil

This, as opposed to the traditional wooden type, is essential for delivering a thin, accurate and consistent line. The cheapest ones will serve just as well as any others, though it's best to get one using 0.5mm leads as these are more commonly available. For marking out, it may be better to use a hard lead such as 2H, but HB is suitable for most other purposes.

Scale rule

The standard three-sided design is the easiest to use, especially if it just displays one scale at a time. Colour coding also helps to locate different scales.

Cutting mat

This serves not only to protect tables and prolong the life of a cutting blade, but also to ensure a non-slip work area. Like the pencil, there is little advantage in getting an expensive one. It should be kept purely for cutting and kept clean; it should not be used for painting or gluing.

Metal ruler

A metal ruler is for measuring but also for cutting against. The best are the simplest; flat strips of steel. The lighter aluminium types (those with the rubber grip) can be too easily damaged. A strip of masking tape along the underside of the simpler type will serve just as well to make it non-slip. It helps to have more than one ruler (preferably 15cm, 30cm and 60cm), because having to wield a long ruler for fine work is both annoying and inaccurate.

Engineers' try square

This is another essential tool for marking out (see Chapter 2). DIY centres will have inexpensive carpenters' try squares, but the smaller metal ones are handier. It is also useful to have an adjustable version, also known as a sliding bevel, for marking off repeated angles.

Metal guide blocks

Unfortunately these can't be bought ready made, but metal stockists may sell offcuts. At least two straight sides are needed, with 90-degree angles (see Chapter 2).

Stanley knife

Although Stanley knives are not suitable for fine cutting, they are useful for some tasks that require a stronger knife. Thin MDF or plywood can often be cut with this knife (especially if the cut is made from both sides).

Fruit knife

The advantage of a fruit knife (which can be found in most kitchen suppliers) over an ordinary penknife for carving soft materials such as styrofoam is that the blade is curved inwards rather than outwards. This makes it easier to shave off thin strips. If used a lot, it is essential to invest in a good sharpening tool.

Saws

The most useful of these is a bead saw, denoting a small blade of thin metal which is reinforced along its upper edge. These are usually fine-toothed and traditional ones (for delicate carpentry) are fixed in a wooden handle. Modern versions often have a detachable plastic handle. Other useful saws for our purposes include a junior hacksaw (for cutting metal) and a coping saw, which has a similar shape and a very slender blade held under tension.

Rasps and files

Most people build up a collection of rasps for wood or files for metal. Model-makers will use them on a variety of materials and all will have some effect. Needle files, for example, are designed for fine work in metal, but they are also excellent for refining details in hardened modelling material. They can also double as soft modelling tools. Rasps or surforms are useful for rough shaping in styrofoam.

Pliers

It is useful to have a few pairs of pliers, including a standard heavy-duty flat nose (preferably with a jaw large enough for bottle tops), a small pair of round-nose pliers (better for bending tight curves in brass rod) and another smaller flat-nose pair with a longer jaw. Although combination pliers include side cutters for snipping wire, it is better to have a separate pair of snippers, or cutting pliers.

Soldering iron

A standard 30W iron is suitable for most model-making purposes, especially if it comes with a choice of bits (*see* Chapter 4). It must have a stand! Antex is a reliable make.

Sandpaper

Any sandpaper will work after a fashion, but sanding will be much more effective if the paper is mounted or at least wrapped around a block, especially when sanding large flat areas. The disposable sandpaper nail files available in chemists are invaluable for delicate work.

Brushes

Apart from the usual selection based on personal preference (ranging from fine and precious to rough and disposable), some special types are necessary. Soft, flat brushes are most useful for dry-brushing effects (*see* Chapter 7). Special brushes are made for stippling paint when using stencils. These are not so suitable for stippling texture as they will clog too quickly and cheap bristle brushes are better. Synthetic brushes may stand up to the rigours of being used incorrectly better than natural hair and are also cheaper. Certain brushes should be reserved (and marked) for particular tasks such as brushing vaseline on prototypes for casting, or applying solvent to styrene (for which natural hair is recommended).

Masking tape

This is a low-tack paper tape used by decorators as a mask before painting. It will hold well, but can be carefully peeled away from most surfaces without damaging them. It is useful for holding down elements while gluing, holding brass in position while soldering or, obviously, for masking areas while painting.

MATERIALS SUPPLIERS

The addresses in this section are grouped first according to speciality and then in order of usefulness, rather than in alphabetical order. Where the company has a permanent website only the general location is given here. It is assumed that you will want to check this first and perhaps make use of online catalogues and mail-order options. Exclusively online suppliers are indicated and grouped under the relevant specialism.

Model shops

4D Modelshop
London E1
www.modelshop.co.uk
There is no better place – or, rather, no other place with the exception of Modulor in Berlin or Tokyu Hands in Japan – where you can find just about everything the professional or hobby model-maker needs under one roof. The time saved often justifies some of the price mark-ups. Also good student discounts and very helpful staff.

Modulor
Berlin
www.modulor.de
Similar to 4D, but specializing more in architecture, product and retail display.

EMA Model Supplies
Online
www.ema-models.com
A major supplier for architectural and product model-makers in particular, offering an extensive range of manufactured forms in plastic (rods, girders, cubes, domes and so on).

Modelzone
London WC1
www.modelzone.co.uk
Mainly model kits, but a small range of materials, tools and paints.

Art and craft suppliers

Tiranti
Thatcham, Berks and London W1
www.tiranti.co.uk
The main, long-established outlet for sculpture materials in London, meeting most of one's needs for carving, modelling, mould-making and casting. Carries a small range of specialist books.

Atlantis Art Materials
London E1
www.atlantisart.co.uk
A large shop with a very extensive range of art materials, often at a more 'student friendly' price. Special features include: a large stock of specialist spray colours; a useful public message board; a wide range of pre-prepared canvases.

Cass Arts
London N1, W1, WC2, W8
www.cass-arts.co.uk
A growing chain of outlets selling competitively priced art materials.

Hobbycraft
Nationwide
www.hobbycraft.co.uk
Art and craft superstore.

Canonbury Arts
London N1
www.canonburyarts.co.uk
A friendly shop selling a good range of art and sculpture materials. Their remit to make non-toxic mould-making and casting materials more available is well worth supporting.

London Graphic Centre
London WC2
www.londongraphics.co.uk
The largest and best organized art shop in Central London, with an emphasis on graphics supplies, but many at Covent Garden prices.

Paperchase
Nationwide
www.paperchase.co.uk
Their mother-ship in London is now a department store filled with a mass of fancy, ephemeral stuff most popular for Christmas and birthdays, but it is still one of the best places in London apart from Falkiner's for its serious range of papers upstairs, especially those supplied by E. Becker. The range of art materials has become sadly rather limited.

Cowling & Wilcox
London W1 and E1
www.cowlingandwilcox.com
Full range of art, craft, graphics and presentation materials. Student discount available.

L. Cornelissen & Son
London WC1
www.cornelissen.com
Long-established supplier of traditional materials and equipment for artists, gilders and specialist decorators.

Paintworks Ltd
London E2
www.paintworks.biz
Competitively priced art materials/framing shop located in the heart of the East end.
Downstairs they have a very good selection of paper and card, one of the best in that area. They often have special deals on job lots of paper. Some sculptural materials for modelling and casting.

The Works
Nationwide
www.theworks.co.uk
A slightly upmarket version of a 'pound shop', with a good though not extensive line in art and craft materials and books. The best place to get packs of cheap brushes and the like.

Specialist Crafts
Online
www.specialistcrafts.co.uk
One of the main suppliers of art and design materials to schools and colleges. It's worth emailing them through the website link to receive a free printed catalogue. It contains most of the basic art materials and books you'd expect, but a lot you might not.

Hindley's
Online
www.hindleys.com
Another supplier to schools, but this time more design and technology oriented, and therefore a much better range of materials such as plastics, metals and wood. Some of the prices, especially for tools, are surprisingly low. A printed catalogue can be requested.

Jackson's Art Supplies
Online
www.jacksonsart.co.uk
Artists' materials and equipment.

Art Discount
Online
www.artdiscount.co.uk
Good deals on art, craft and educational materials.

Do-it-yourself

B&Q
www.diy.com
The size and quality varies according to location. Useful timber-cutting services.

Travis Perkins Building Supplies
www.travisperkins.co.uk
Often the cheapest source for materials used in building, such as polyfilla or styrofoam.

Wickes
www.wickes.co.uk
Building and decorating supplies.

Machine Mart
www.machinemart.co.uk
The biggest range of tools imaginable. No materials, just tools. Order online if you know what you want, or visit your local store.

Specialist suppliers

Abplas
London SW19
www.abplas.co.uk
A small and friendly shop stocking a good range of plastics including foamed PVC, styrene, acrylic and Perspex.

Hamar Acrylic Fabrications
London E2
www.hamaracrylic.co.uk
Mainly acrylic plastics in sheet form or custom makes.

GPX Group
Online
www.glazerplastics.co.uk
Suppliers of plastic sheeting, for example PVC and acrylic.

Robert Horne Group
www.roberthorne.co.uk
Large paper, board and plastics supplier.

British Plastics Federation
www.bpf.co.uk
Although not a retail source, it will list suppliers of different kinds of plastic and provides a lot of detailed information.

Falkiner Fine Papers
London WC1
www.falkiners.com
Excellent range of quality papers of just about every type imaginable. Browse through sample books, or ask the knowledgeable staff.

Scientific Wire Company
London E18
www.wires.co.uk
The most comprehensive and often the cheapest source for any kind of wire. Mainly mail order through a small catalogue rather than 'browsing'.

Pentonville Rubber
London N1
www.pentonvillerubber.co.uk
A good source for soft foams and plastazote.

Bentley Chemicals
www.bentleychemicals.co.uk
One of the main suppliers to the British film and theatre industry of silicones, polyurethanes and resins for mould-making, casting and prosthetics. You can't buy from them, but they will list London stockists and offer technical advice. The 4D Modelshop is one of their official stockists, albeit with a limited range on its shelves. The Bentley website is worth looking at first to see the range and collect some technical know-how. The handiest range to look at, in terms of fitting the simple requirements of the model-maker or sculptor, is the one from Smooth-on. Bentley is always very helpful with technical queries.

Mouldlife
www.mouldlife.co.uk
Specialist distributors of mould-making silicone rubbers and polyurethane resins for casting.

Flint Hire & Supply Ltd
London SE17
www.flints.co.uk
Well-established London theatre supplier with a good range of scenic materials, paints and so on.

Maplin Electronics
Nationwide
www.maplin.co.uk
Relevant here for metal etching or soldering materials, but worth browsing for other things.

MacCulloch and Wallis
London W1
www.macculloch-wallis.co.uk
Fabrics and haberdashery. A good selection of ribbons, trimmings and so on.

Borovick Fabrics
London W1
www.borovickfabricsltd.co.uk
A busy rag trade and theatrical fabric shop which is sometimes worth going into just for the banter!

The Bead Shop
www.beadshop.co.uk
London WC2
The most useful things are the findings, small bits like clasps or mounts which sometimes function well as parts of furniture or chandelier decoration.

Sewing & Craft Superstore
London SW17
www.craftysewer.com
Fabrics and fabric craft materials.

London Metal Company
Morden, Surrey
www.londonmetal.co.uk
For all metal requirements, such as steel, stainless steel, aluminium, brass and copper, but not necessarily in small gauges or amounts.

Russell & Chapple Ltd 'The Specialists in Canvas'
London WC2
www.russellandchapple.co.uk
Canvas specialists, also stocking a range of art and theatrical supplies.

BIBLIOGRAPHY

This is a selection of books relevant to (or featuring) models and model-making. It is not intended to be comprehensive.

Practical books on model-making

Jackson, Albert and Day, David, *The Modelmaker's Handbook* (Random House, 1981).

Mills, Criss B., *Designing with Models: A Studio Guide to Making and Using Architectural Design Models* (John Wiley & Sons, 2005).

Orton, Keith, *Model Making for the Stage* (The Crowood Press, 2004).

Payne, Christopher, *The Encyclopaedia of Modelmaking Techniques* (Diane Publishing Co., 2003).

Schilling, Alexander, *Modelbuilding* (Birkhauser Verlag, 2006).

Sutherland, Martha, *Model Making: A Basic Guide* (Norton Professional Books for Architects, 1999).

Trudeau, Norman, *Professional Modelmaking: A Handbook of Techniques and Materials for Architects and Designers* (Watson-Guptill, 1995).

Practical books on related subjects

Brooks, Nick, *Mouldmaking and Casting* (The Crowood Press, 2005).

Cain, Tubal, *Soldering and Brazing* (Special Interest Model Books, 1998).

Davenport, John, *Making Miniature Furniture* (Batsford, 1997).

Hebborn, Eric, *The Art Forger's Handbook* (Overlook Press, 2004).

John, *Making Miniature Furniture* (Batsford, 1997).

James, Thurston, *The Prop Builder's Molding & Casting Handbook* (North Light Books, 1990).

King, Brian, *Photo Etching* (Special Interest Model Books, 2005).

Langland, Tuck, *From Clay to Bronze: A Studio Guide to Figurative Sculpture* (Watson-Guptill, 1999).

Lammas, David, *Adhesives and Sealants* (Special Interest Model Books, 1998).

Lanteri, Edouard, *Modelling and Sculpting the Human Figure* (Dover, 1986).

Mills, John W., *Encyclopaedia of Sculpture Techniques* (Batsford, 2005).

Plowman, John, *The Sculptor's Bible: The All-media Reference to Surface Effects and How to Achieve Them* (A & C Black, 2005).

Scutts, Jerry (ed.), *Modelling and Painting Figures* (Osprey, 2000).

Shaw, Susannah, *Stop Motion: Craft Skills for Model Animation* (Focal Press, 2004).

Windrow, Richard, *Advanced Terrain Modelling* (Osprey, 2007).

Windrow, Richard, *Terrain Modelling* (Osprey, 2001).

Books on models

Boyer, Hatton and Weingartner, Fannia, *Miniature Rooms: The Thorne Rooms at the Art Institute of Chicago* (Art Institute of Chicago, 2005).

Kurrent, Friedrich (ed.), *Scale Models: Houses of the 20th Century* (Birkhauser Verlag, 1999).

Morris, Mark, *Models: Architecture and the Miniature* (Wiley-Academy, 2006).

Porter, Tom and Neale, John, *Architectural Supermodels* (Architectural Press, 2000).

Quinn, Stephen Christopher, *Windows on Nature* (Harry N. Abrams, 2006).

Rugoff, Ralph and Kamps, Toby, *Small World: Dioramas in Contemporary Art* (San Diego Museum of Contemporary Art, 2000).

Visual reference books

Calloway, S., *The Elements of Style: An Encyclopaedia of Domestic Architectural Details* (Mitchell Beazley, 1991).

Huntley, Michael, *A History of Furniture: Ancient to 19thC* (Guild of Master Craftsman Publications, 2004).

Jones, Owen, *The Grammar of Ornament* (Dover, 1988).

Juracek, Judy A. and Hayward, Gordon, *Natural Surfaces: Visual Research for Artists, Architects and Designers* (Thames & Hudson, 2002).

Juracek, Judy A., *Architectural Surfaces: Details for Architects, Designers and Artists* (Thames & Hudson, 2006).

Meyer, Franz Sales, *Handbook of Ornament* (Dover, 2000).

Miller, Judith, *Period Details Sourcebook* (Mitchell Beazley, 1999).

Miller, Judith, *The Style Sourcebook: The Definitive Visual Directory of Fabrics, Wallpapers, Paints, Flooring and Tiles* (Mitchell Beazley, 2003).

Speltz, Alexander, *The Styles of Ornament* (Dover, 2000).

Thornton, Peter, *Authentic Decor: The Domestic Interior 1620–1920* (Weidenfeld Nicolson, 2000).

Useful books on specific disciplines

Ettedgui, Peter, *Production Design and Art Direction* (Focal Press, 1999).

Harryhausen, Ray and Dalton, Tony, *Ray Harryhausen: An Animated Life* (Aurum Press, 2003).

Peterson, Lorne, *Sculpting a Galaxy: Inside the 'Star Wars' Model Shop* (Insight Editions, 2006).

Rickitt, Richard, *Special Effects: The History and Technique* (Billboard Books, 2007).

Sawicki, Mark, *Filming the Fantastic: A Guide to Visual Effects Cinematography* (Focal Press, 2007).

Thorne, Gary, *Stage Design: A Practical Guide* (The Crowood Press, 1999).

Winslow, Colin, *The Handbook of Set Design* (The Crowood Press, 2006).

Websites

A range of useful websites can be quickly found using one's own keyword search, so the following are just some examples.

www.artquest.org.uk University of the Arts, London information resources for artists and craftspeople.

www.diydata.com Practical information for DIY, most useful for its advice on paints, glues and solvents.

www.materialworks.com Practical and technical information on a wide range of materials.

www.modelshop.co.uk The website of 4D Modelshop, London. In addition to the online catalogue there is a database of freelance model-makers, model-making courses, jobs and online tutorials.

www.themodelmakersresource.co.uk Created for the kit or terrain enthusiast, but many useful and clearly written tutorials on a variety of subjects.

INDEX